THE AARON WILDAVSKY FORUM FOR PUBLIC POLICY

Edited by Lee Friedman

This series is intended to sustain the intellectual excitement that Aaron Wildavsky created for scholars of public policy everywhere. The ideas in each volume are initially presented and discussed at a public lecture and forum held at the University of California.

1. *Missing Persons: A Critique of Personhood in the Social Sciences*, by Mary Douglas and Steven Ney
2. *The Bridge over the Racial Divide: Rising Inequality and Coalition Politics*, by William Julius Wilson
3. *The New Public Management: Improving Research and Policy Dialogue*, by Michael Barzelay

Aaron Wildavsky, 1930–1993

"Your prolific pen has brought real politics to the study of budgeting, to the analysis of myriad public policies, and to the discovery of the values underlying the political cultures by which peoples live. You have improved every institution with which you have been associated, notably Berkeley's Graduate School of Public Policy, which as Founding Dean you quickened with your restless innovative energy. Advocate of freedom, mentor of policy analysts everywhere."

(Yale University, May 1993, from text granting the honorary degree of Doctor of Social Science)

THE NEW PUBLIC MANAGEMENT

THE NEW PUBLIC MANAGEMENT

Improving Research and Policy Dialogue

Michael Barzelay

UNIVERSITY OF CALIFORNIA PRESS

Berkeley *Los Angeles* *London*

RUSSELL SAGE FOUNDATION

New York

University of California Press
Berkeley and Los Angeles, California
University of California Press, Ltd.
Oxford, England

Library of Congress Cataloging-in-Publication Data
Barzelay, Michael.

The new public management : improving research and policy dialogue / Michael Barzelay.
p. cm.—(The Aaron Wildavsky Forum for public policy ; 3)
Includes bibliographical references and index.
ISBN 0-520-22443-4 (cloth : alk. paper)
1. Public administration. I. Title. II. Series.

JF1351 .B28 2001
351—dc21 00-055168

Printed in the United States of America
08 07 06 05 04 03 02 01
10 9 8 7 6 5 4 3 2 1

The paper used in this publication is both acid-free and totally chlorine-free (TCF). It meets the minimum requirement of ANSI/NISO Z39.48-1992 (R 1997) *(Permanence of Paper)*

For Catherine

CONTENTS

FIGURES AND BOXES

FIGURES

BOXES

PREFACE

The New Public Management (NPM) is a shorthand expression regularly used by scholars and professionals to refer to distinctive themes, styles, and patterns of public service management that have come to the fore within the past two decades, notably in the United Kingdom, Australia, and New Zealand. The term first appeared in the academic literature in the early 1990s and quickly caught on. Scholars widely agree that NPM exists; what the phrase "really means" is, however, a matter of controversy.

The original view held NPM to be a body of doctrinal beliefs that had discredited Progressive Public Administration's answers to administrative what-to-do questions in government and that had established itself as an accepted administrative philosophy (Hood 1991). NPM's acceptance, by this argument, was due to the rhetoric of "econocrats" and "consultocrats" (Hood and Jackson 1991). A variant of this view is that NPM is a set of highly mobile ideas about public management that have spread rapidly from source countries, for example, New Zealand, to countries all over the globe (Boston 1996; Kettl 1997). However, a contrasting perspective holds that NPM is a valid framework for making decisions about how to structure and manage the public service (Aucoin 1995). This policy framework is based on theoretical ideas about organization and management that have established a mainstream position in the economics profession as well as political science (Boston 1991; Stiglitz 1994; Horn 1995). Finally, there is the view that NPM is an empirical style of organizing public services (Hood 1994), exemplified by the construction of "quasi-markets" in the health and education sectors (Robinson and LeGrand 1993) yet also encompassing changes in government-wide systems of financial management, personnel management, procurement, and auditing (Schick 1996).

The NPM literature is impressive to the extent that policy-level issues of public management are being given significant attention by scholars grounded in several academic and professional disciplines. However, a weak point of NPM is that scholarship on this subject has gone off in many directions—a tendency even within some individual works. The result, for me, is mixed feelings about the NPM literature and uncertainty about its potential scholarly achievement and practical utility.

This book proceeds on the basis of three key beliefs about how to improve the field. The first is that the NPM phenomenon needs to be analyzed in parts rather than holistically. The second is that empirical research seeking to *explain* governments' handling of policy-level issues of public management needs to be better carried out. The third is that the substantive analysis of

NPM requires a genuinely interdisciplinary dialogue that has so far been in short supply.

My effort to improve the NPM literature through this book is twofold. The primary effort is to draw on the discipline of political science to improve the empirical research literature on one major aspect of NPM, that is, what I call public management policy-making. This aspect of NPM relates to changing government-wide institutional rules through which public service organizations are guided, controlled, and motivated. These institutional rules can be subdivided into the traditional categories of expenditure planning and financial management, civil service and labor relations, procurement, organization and methods, and audit and evaluation. My narrow aim in focusing on this part of NPM in chapters 2 and 3 is to explain public management policy choices. My slightly broader aim is to demonstrate that political science can make a larger contribution to the NPM research literature than is generally recognized.

The secondary effort is to overcome factors that undermine the potential for scholarly discussion of NPM to evolve into a genuinely interdisciplinary conversation about what-to-do questions in public management. One clear limiting factor is that economics and public administration remain "knowledge enclaves," a generalization that admits to some notable exceptions (Horn 1995; Schick 1996). Providing an intellectual strategy to eliminate this constraint is the aim of chapters 4 and 5.

These two efforts boil down to a call for public management to become a vibrant field of public policy in the sense the term was originally understood in schools of public policy in the United States. Vibrant fields of public policy provide a home to empirical research on the politics of policy-making as well as to sophisticated, interdisciplinary dialogue on what-to-do questions (Wildavsky 1979; Fleishman 1990; Lynn 1996; Dunn 1994). Public management, in sum, should become a proper field of public policy. I suspect that Aaron Wildavsky (whose memory is honored by this book) would have been sympathetic to this point; I know he could have put it better.

ACKNOWLEDGMENTS

I am immeasurably grateful for the honor of presenting a lecture on public management at the University of California, Berkeley, in the memory of Aaron Wildavsky, who was a commanding figure in the fields of political science, public administration, and public policy. The organizers of the Wildavsky Forum for Public Policy took a risk in inviting a less than fully established scholar to deliver it. (The preceding speakers in the Wildavsky Forum were Mary Douglas and William Julius Wilson.) Not all major U.S. universities would have been inclined to incur such a risk.

The interval between the extension of the invitation and the delivery of the lecture was four years. In the middle of this interval, I moved from Harvard's John F. Kennedy School of Government to the London School of Economics and Political Science, where I took up a new joint appointment between the Government Department and the Interdisciplinary Institute of Management. The move has made an enormous difference to the present project for many reasons, not least being the fact that LSE is a research-oriented university where public administration is a core field of political science and where concern for public management rivals that for private management.

Through my teaching activities and collegial interactions within the Government Department, I have come to appreciate the contribution that political science research can make to the field of public management. Similarly, my time in LSE's Interdisciplinary Institute of Management has exposed me to approaches to management taken by specialists in the economics of organization. The selection and treatment of topics in this volume reflects this environment at LSE. Although my appointment to the LSE academic staff was an institutional act, I would particularly like to acknowledge the efforts made before, and the collegiality extended since, by Christopher Hood, the Professor of Public Administration and Public Policy, and by Professor Peter Abell, Director of the Interdisciplinary Institute of Management. Hood's work on the New Public Management provided a crucial benchmark for this entire effort, and Abell's suggestions for methodological development proved essential.

The Wildavsky lecture, delivered at Berkeley in April 1997, was an important milestone in the long journey toward completing this book. A session held on the following day to discuss the lecture conveyed three messages: the topic was a good choice; I was proceeding in a sensible way; and I was in utter denial of how big a project I had taken on. For these messages, as well as for more detailed comments, I am grateful to the appointed discussants—Peter Evans of Berkeley's Sociology Department and Martin Landau of the Political Science Department—as well as to several participants in the same session, including Eugene

Bardach, John Ellwood, Lee Friedman, Larry Jones, George Lakoff, Nelson Polsby, and Fred Thompson.

The International Public Management Network (IPMN), organized in 1996 by Larry Jones, Kuno Schedler, and Fred Thompson, has also been instrumental in shaping this book. The IPMN is a venue for presenting research on topics relating to New Public Management as well as for conducting interdisciplinary dialogue. Network members are mainly based in Europe, North America, Australia, and New Zealand, and their disciplinary identities include accounting and control, public administration, public policy, management, economics, and political science. The first IPMN research conference, held in Switzerland at the University of St. Gallen in 1996, convinced me to tie my Wildavsky lecture to the subject of NPM while helping me envision an audience for this book. I presented a revised version of my Wildavsky lecture at the 1997 IPMN research workshop held in Germany at Potsdam University. Hellmut Wollman's comments on that occasion were especially helpful. Interactions with IPMN colleagues from fields other than my own, especially management control, led me to formulate my ideas on interdisciplinary dialogue, which I presented at the 1998 IPMN research conference held at the Atkinson Graduate School of Management, Willamette University in Salem, Oregon. For their professional collegiality, I am especially grateful to IPMN members Sanford Borins, Howard Frant, James Guthrie, Nathalie Halgand, Larry Jones, Rob Laking, Elke Löffler, Riccardo Mussari, June Pallot, Christoph Reichard, Alasdair Roberts, Kuno Schedler, and Fred Thompson.

I have benefited from several other occasions when I was asked to present my work in progress and to discuss it with academic colleagues. These occasions included delivering a keynote address at the annual Congress of the revitalized Latin American Center for Public Administration and Development (CLAD) held on Isla Marguerita, Venezuela, and presenting at a conference on Managerial Reform of the State held in Brasília to mark the fiftieth anniversary of the United Nations program on public administration. For arranging for these two opportunities to interact with academic colleagues, drawn mainly from Latin America and Europe, I would like to extend particular thanks to Luiz Carlos Bresser Pereira, then Brazil's Minister of Federal Administration and Reform of the State as well as a professor of management at the Fundação Getúlio Vargas, São Paulo.

In December 1998, a memorable discussion of a draft of this book was held in Barcelona at a seminar organized jointly by the Institute of Public Management (IDGP) of ESADE, the Faculty of Political Science and Public Law of the Universitat Autònoma de Barcelona, and the Universitat Pompeu Fabra. I particularly appreciated the comments of the appointed discussants, Peter Knopfel of the Institute de Hautes Etudes d'Administration Publique in Lausanne and Quim Brugué of the Universitat Autònoma de Barcelona, as well as those of seminar participants Koldo Echebarria, Raquel Gallego-Calderón, Miguel Angel Lasheras, Les Metcalfe, Antonio Porras, and Joan Subirats. Closer to home, I also benefited substantially from presenting this work at an LSE Government Department Staff Seminar in March 1999. The comments of Patrick Dunleavy were particularly challenging and therefore helpful.

As most academics know, the most intense source of encouragement and criticism received in writing a scholarly book are doctoral students. In this context, I would particularly like to thank Anne Corbett, Francisco Gaetani, Raquel Gallego-Calderón, Bryan Hassel, and Florian Lennert. I owe a particular word of thanks to Raquel Gallego-Calderón. In commenting on my initial sketch of the Wildavsky lecture, she delivered a devastating critique of the New Public Management literature on which my lecture was to be based. Working out a constructive response to Raquel's no-holds-barred critique of NPM as an intellectual construct has been a thrust of this research and writing effort.

For helpful comments on various drafts of the manuscript, I am grateful to Marshall Bailey, Eugene Bardach, Colin Campbell, Anne Corbett, Patrick Field, Natascha Fuechtner, Francisco Gaetani, Nathalie Halgand, Peter Hall, Stephen Hill, Larry Jones, Jan-Erik Lane, Charles E. Lindblom, Jeroen Maesschalck, Alex Matheson, James Montgomery, Salvador Parrado Diez, Celina Souza, Sascha Spoun, Fred Thompson, and two anonymous referees appointed by the University of California Press. Campbell was especially helpful in commenting on several drafts of chapter 3, while Montgomery provided insights into principal agent theory and its relevance, as discussed in chapter 4.

I had to pass many milestones on the way to being satisfied with this project and to enjoy working on it. No one outside my family and close circle of friends knows this fact more than Helen Perry, who has assisted me since receiving her doctorate from LSE in 1996. I have been extremely fortunate in having been able to draw on her scholarly judgment, research skills, and editorial finesse for four years.

The entreaties of my young children, Adèle and Alexandre, to play and read with them have had the effect of increasing the opportunity cost of working on this project. The reader can give them some credit for my writing a short book. The credit for its being written at all, however, goes to my wife, Catherine Moukheibir. As part of our moving to London, she has shouldered burdens that would easily crush anyone else. Dedicating *this* book to her is particularly fitting, since it is my first that she has not discussed incessantly, edited repeatedly, and otherwise brought to completion.

CHAPTER ONE

Studying the New Public Management

For much of the twentieth century, policy debates about administration and management in government took place within narrow bandwidths, at least among the developed democracies. The once contentious political and policy questions about the role and structure of public bureaucracy were substantially settled. In the affluent post-war era of governmental expansion, public administration and management essentially receded to the background, with attention focused instead on such policy issues as national security, economic performance, social security, and health and safety. Public management was generally regarded as a process through which policies were formulated, resources allocated, and programs implemented, rather than as a policy issue in its own right.

However, beginning in the 1970s, the potential for policy change in the area of public management increased, as economies suffered stagflation and public perceptions of bureaucracy became more negative. During her tenure as prime minister of the United Kingdom, Margaret Thatcher successfully made the culture, size, cost, and operation of the British civil service a policy issue. Playing the functional role of "policy entrepreneur" (Kingdon 1984), as well as the official role of prime minister, Thatcher drove through changes in public management policies in such areas as organization and methods, civil service and labor relations, expenditure planning and financial management, audit and evaluation, and procurement. Her successor, John Major, kept public management policy high on the formal agenda of the Conservative government, leading to the implementation of the Next Steps Initiative and the launching of the Citizens Charter Initiative, Competing for Quality, Resource Accounting and Budgeting, and the Private Finance Initiative.

In the 1980s, public management became an active area of policy-making in numerous other countries, notably in New Zealand, Australia, and Sweden. At the same time, the Organization for Economic Cooperation and Development (OECD) established its Public Management Committee and Secretariat (PUMA), conferring to public management the status normally accorded more conventional domains of policy. In the 1990s, public management was a major item on President Clinton's agenda. Early policy actions of the Clinton administration included launching the National Performance Review and signing into law the Government Performance and Results Act. At the time of this writing, there are few indications that public management issues will vanish from governmental policy agendas any time soon.

The term *New Public Management* (NPM) expresses the idea that the cumulative flow of policy decisions over the past twenty years has amounted to a substantial shift in the governance and management of the "state sector" in the United Kingdom, New Zealand, Australia, Scandinavia, and North America. A benign interpretation is that these decisions have been a defensible, if imperfect, response to policy problems. Those problems as well as their solutions were formulated within the policy-making process. The agenda-setting process, in particular, has been heavily influenced by electoral commitments to improve macroeconomic performance and to contain growth in the public sector, as well as by a growing perception of public bureaucracies as being inefficient. The alternative-generation process has been heavily influenced by ideas coming from economics and from various quarters within the field of management.

THE NPM LITERATURE

Expertise on the New Public Management is claimed by scholars based in public administration, accounting and control, management, economics, and public policy. Specialists in public administration often focus on how NPM relates to budgeting, financial management, civil service and labor relations, procurement, organization and methods, and audit and evaluation. Specialists in accounting are especially concerned with adapting techniques of management control, including performance measurement, to government organizations. Specialists in organizational economics apply their highly codified theoretical ideas and signature skills of analysis to evaluate institutional forms within the state sector. Specialists in sector-specific or substantive policy areas—such as health, policing, social services, and defense—also write on NPM as it relates to program design and operation in their particular areas.

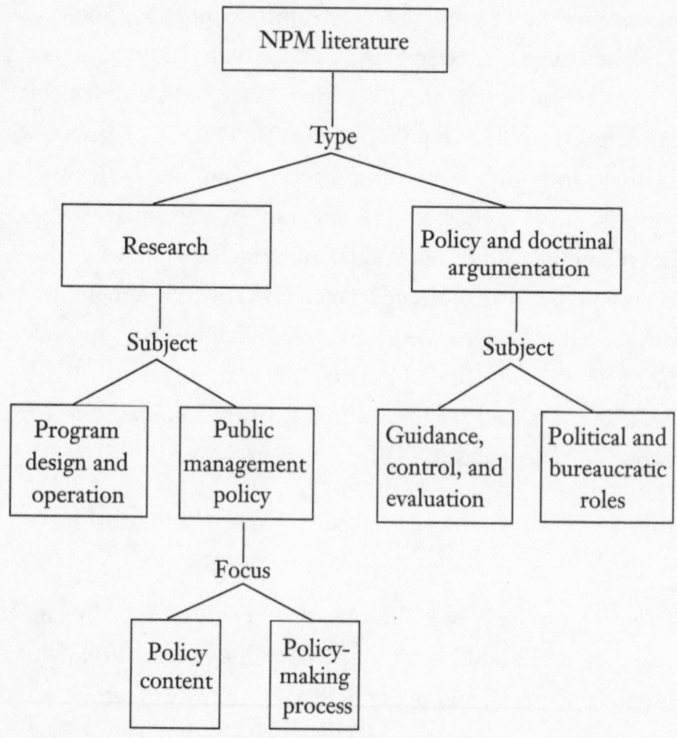

Figure 1. Schema of the NPM Literature

The NPM literature as a whole is amorphous, as might be expected of an interdisciplinary, policy-oriented field. Figure 1 is an attempt to give the NPM literature a recognizable shape. This scheme divides the NPM literature into two main branches: research and argumentation. "Research" refers to scholarly works intended to explain facts and events (Elster 1989). An illustrative fact is the negative tone of public discussion of bureaucracy in many countries; an illustrative event is the Clinton administration's launching of the U.S. National Performance Review in

1993. "Argumentation" refers to scholarly dialogues about what-to-do ideas and actual policies concerning government, policy, and management. Contributions to these dialogues often resolve, reformulate, or incite doctrinal controversies, for example, over the role of accounting information systems and performance measurement systems in government.

Research on Program Design and Operation

The major branch labeled *research* is subdivided into two major subject areas, the first of which is program design and operation. Programs are packages of activity intended to "create public value" (Moore 1995) by addressing problems in such areas as health, criminal justice, education, employment, and economic development. Program design involves the crafting of institutional roles and frameworks through which policy tools are deployed (Hood 1986; Salamon 1989). Numerous works within the NPM research literature discuss and analyze changes in program design in one or more programmatic areas. For instance, a volume edited by Robinson and LeGrand (1993) analyzes the shift in policy tools employed in British social programs under the rubric of constructing "quasi-markets." Ferlie et al. (1996) describe and analyze intended and actual changes in the institutional roles and frameworks of the British National Health Service.

Illustrative scholarly works on program operation are Sparrow (1994) and Bardach (1998). Sparrow describes and analyzes changes in the operation of programs falling within the areas of environmental protection, policing, and revenue administration. NPM in this context would refer to the development of innovative practiced routines that are intended to improve the performance of compliance or enforcement programs. Bardach describes and analyzes efforts to achieve sustained collaboration among street-level bureaucrats who operate different social programs. NPM in this context would refer to the development of practiced routines for achieving unity of effort despite inhibiting institutional rules.

Research on Public Management Policy

The second major research subject area is what I call public management policy. Public management policies are authoritative means intended to guide, constrain, and motivate the public service as a whole. Historically, the immediate targets of public management policy have included procedures for staffing the public service, planning organizational activity, buying supplies from industry, disbursing public funds, changing organizational structures, and communicating with the public and legislature. The recent history of public management policy in many countries—not least the United Kingdom, Australia, and New Zealand—involves intended and actual changes in the institutional rules and routines constituting public management policies.

The literature on public management policy subdivides into two types: works that focus on policy content and those that focus on the policy process. The first type describes procedures, usually contrasted with previous practice. An example is Boston et al.'s *Public Management: The New Zealand Model* (1996). Works of this type are sometimes comparative; a fine example is Löffler's (1996) monograph describing the structure and operation of quality awards programs in a dozen or so countries.

The second type of research on public management policy goes beyond description to explain policy events, such as the launch of the United Kingdom's Next Steps Initiative, as well as facts, such as the degree to which procedures have actually changed. An example is Campbell and Halligan's (1992) study of how Australia's cabinet and central coordinating agencies under prime ministers Hawke and Keating propelled change in government-wide managerial systems, including systems of budget formulation, financial management, civil service, and industrial relations. By way of description, Campbell and Halligan catalog major policy events related to public management (such as the merger of departments and reshuffling of missions), identify influential policy ideas (such as "economic rationalism"), track the implementation of policy initiatives (such as the Financial Management Improvement Program), and calibrate how much change eventually took place. By way of explanation, the authors consider such factors as executive leadership skills of the prime minister, policy spillovers driven by doctrines of economic rationalism, and bureaucratic competence within central agencies. This single case study is an excellent example of research on the dynamics of the public management policy-making process.[1]

Argumentation

The second main branch of the NPM literature is policy and doctrinal argumentation (see top of Figure 1). A useful analytic division is between works focusing on political and bureaucratic roles, on one hand, and guidance, control, and evaluation processes, on the other. Moore's (1995) *Creating Public Value: Strategic Management in Government* is an excellent example of the former. Moore illustrates and defends an argument about what executives and managers in government should do ("create public value") and how they should do it (by "managing strategically"). In terms of its subject matter, the second category under argumentation relates closely to public management policy. Aucoin's (1995) *New Public Management* exemplifies this subcategory, since it engages doctrinal as well as policy arguments about the design of mechanisms for guiding and controlling public organizations.

Aucoin described NPM as a network of claims, including the following: elected executives should resolve ambiguity, uncertainty, and conflict surrounding public policy in order to specify *in advance* what they want their officials to accomplish within a given time frame; the functions of policy-making and operations should be assigned to different organizations, with operational organizations headed by officials who are adept at managing; and centralized administrative systems should be revamped to devolve responsibility, authority, and accountability down the line. Aucoin argued that policies styled along these lines are able to overcome problems of executive fragmentation and administrative centralization, key impediments to governance and public sector performance in the 1970s. Addressing critics of NPM, Aucoin argues that such policies are not only effective, but that the underlying doctrines are appropriate in being consistent with norms for governing public bureaucracies in Westminster systems. As a closely reasoned essay that relates to much previous writing on the subject, Aucoin's book is exemplary of this subtype of argumentation.

Since the classificatory scheme pictured in Figure 1 imposes form on the otherwise amorphous NPM literature, the usual caveats apply. The relationship between particular works and locations within the scheme is not one-to-one: some works include both research and argumentation (e.g., Barzelay 1992; Savoie 1994; Aucoin 1995), while some authors assimilate program design and operation with public management policy (e.g., Hood 1994; Schwartz 1994a, 1994b).

This book seeks to contribute specifically to the NPM literature on public management policy, in terms of both research and argumentation. As I have pointed out, public management policies are government-wide institutional rules and routines in the areas of expenditure planning and financial management, civil service and labor relations, procurement, organization and methods, and audit and evaluation. The division of labor is as follows: chapters 2 and 3 contribute to research on the public management policy-making process, while chapters 4 and 5 focus on argumentation about guidance, control, and evaluation.

IMPROVING RESEARCH AND ARGUMENTATION

NPM has been understood as a trend exemplified by the United Kingdom, New Zealand, and Australia. The idea that NPM is an international trend was stimulated by two seminal articles, by Peter Aucoin (1990) and Christopher Hood (1991). This view has since become commonplace in professional discussions. The idea that NPM is a trend is not conducive to research progress, however, for two main reasons. First, it places a premium on discerning similarities among cases; and second, it tends to cast explanations in terms of driving forces, such as fiscal stress, acceptance of ideas, and technological innovation. Pinpointing a trend is not the same as conducting public policy research on a comparative basis.

In this volume, the choice of what is to be explained, and how, is substantially guided by empirical research traditions in political science. Case-oriented comparative research seeks to explain differences among cases, no less than their similarities (Ragin 1987), and public policy research identifies precise mechanisms that link macro influences (such as fiscal stress) to concrete policy decisions (Kingdon 1984; Hedström and Swedberg 1998).[2] Shifting the emphasis of NPM scholarship from trend spotting to policy research is arguably long overdue.[3]

The intellectual aim pursued in chapters 2 and 3 is to explain changes in public management policy. This aim is different from the explanation of changes in accepted public management ideas, which has been a central concern of explanatory studies about NPM (Hood and Jackson 1991). Ideas enter the discussion here as explanatory factors; their effects are mediated by issue images, structures affecting participation in decision making, alternative courses of action considered, evaluations of past policy choices, and the like. To reiterate, the outcomes to be explained are policy choices, not styles or themes or other characteristic descriptions of the New Public Management.

Chapter 2 reviews the case study literature on public management policy change in Australia, the United Kingdom, the United States, Canada, Germany, and Sweden. Chapter 3 uses case-oriented research methods to develop generalizations about public management policy-making. These methods are first applied to cases that are emblematic of the New Public Management: the United Kingdom, Australia, and New Zealand. The designated case outcome to be explained is across-the-board change in institutional rules covering expenditure planning and financial management, civil service and labor relations, procurement, organization and methods, and audit and evaluation. The same method is deployed to account for more limited change in Germany within the same time frame. Explaining case similarities and differences is a basis for developing limited historical generalizations about public management policy-making.[4]

The empirical analysis indicates that across-the-board change in public management policy can be attributed to the combined effect of changes in issue image, domain, and jurisdiction—specifically:

- the acceptance of the idea that governmental organizations are inefficient;
- the unification of the public management policy domain, with institutional rules affecting money, people, and procedures viewed as components of a system to be influenced through public management policy; and
- the broadening of the jurisdiction of budget-related central agencies to include significant responsibility for public management policy as a whole.

These changes were influenced by a combination of other factors, including noninstitutional ones—such as economic policy reversals and the presence of arguments based on public choice and managerialist presumptions—and institutional ones—such as parliamentary systems, single party governments, and the initial roles and responsibilities of central agencies.

Such knowledge is potentially useful for policy-makers as they analyze the prospects and conditions for public management policy change. At a minimum, analysts will become sensitized to such causal factors as the image of an inefficient public service, a broad-based domain of public management policy-making, and the potential for central staff agencies to serve as an institutional base for policy entrepreneurship. On this basis, judgments about the feasibility of policy change can be informed by research.

The presumption that NPM exemplars such as the United Kingdom and New Zealand are worthy of widespread emulation is often the basis of discussions in professional and official circles. The framing of NPM as a trend encourages this presumption; its acceptance encourages policy-making through imitation rather than problem solving.[5] The analysis of public management policies, therefore, requires a substantive, in addition to a processual, discussion.

The works selected for attention in chapters 4 and 5 develop systematic arguments about the desirability of particular public management policies. Some of the works discussed in this part of the book are highly favorable toward the New Public Management; others are much less so. The question is why. The analysis of these arguments indicates that evaluations hinge on the particular theory of public management policy the author employs. Some authors draw heavily on the new institutional economics, others on fields of management, and still others on empirical theories of the governmental process. Public administration scholars, unlike economists, have yet to develop a common framework for analyzing public management policies.

As a way forward, this book attempts to provide a mode of policy dialogue that does not rely exclusively on the new institutional economics. To this end, chapter 4, entitled "How to Argue about the New Public Management," provides guidelines for argumentation about public management policy. To illustrate, one guideline is to distinguish theories of public management policy from evaluations of practice. Another guideline is to present arguments in a quasi-formal manner, so that readers can readily discern their broad structure. The use of such tools can benefit scholarly communication among public administrationists, in particular.[6] A third guideline is to take semantics seriously. Deploying tools of conceptual analysis is essential to clarifying disagreement and cumulating insights, as will be demonstrated in chapters 4 and 5. The case for following these guidelines rests on fundamental concepts of practical argumentation as well as on the relative absence of policy dialogue about NPM.

In sum, although the idea of NPM has promoted international scholarly discussion of public management, neither research nor doctrinal and policy argumentation on this subject are wholly satisfactory as yet. The concluding chapter summarizes this book's proposal for improving research and policy dialogue about public management policy—the aspect of NPM considered here. This proposal, as will be easily recognized, is deeply rooted in the intellectual tradition that Aaron Wildavsky advanced throughout his abundantly productive scholarly career.

CHAPTER TWO

Case Studies on Public Management Policy-Making

This chapter reviews the empirical research literature on public management policy-making in selected countries during the 1980s and 1990s. The contributors to the literature reviewed are mainly academic public administrationists and political scientists specializing in executive government. The criteria for inclusion in this review are as follows.

First, the primary subject matter must be public management policy-making in central or federal governments. Public management policy is defined here as the sum of institutional rules that guide, constrain, and motivate the public service as a whole. Public management policies belong to such established categories as expenditure planning and financial management, civil service and labor relations, procurement, organization and methods, and audit and evaluation. Accordingly, works that are mainly concerned with program design and operation (e.g., Ferlie et al. 1996) are excluded from discussion.

Second, included works identify and explain particular policy events and/or implementation outcomes. Works whose main aims are to describe and offer policy commentary, but not to explain, are excluded, such as Metcalfe and Richards (1987), Boston et al. (1991, 1996), Pollitt (1993), Moe (1994), McSweeney (1994), Humphrey and Olson (1995), Schick (1996), Power (1997), and Clarke and Newman (1997). This criterion also led to exclusion of studies that explain stylized facts—rather than policy events or outcomes—about the New Public Management, such as Meyer (1983), Dunleavy (1991), and Hood and Jackson (1994).

As most of the works that meet these two criteria focus on either one or two country cases, the chapter has been organized by country. The survey begins with Australia and then continues with the United Kingdom, the United States, Canada, Sweden, and Germany. The concluding section considers prospects for research progress, if the literature proceeds along the present lines.

In writing this review, I have placed emphasis on the works' explanatory argument; in the process, I may have put words into the mouths of several fellow scholars. I claim poetic license in the interest of demonstrating that a coherent descriptive and explanatory literature on public management policy-making is beginning to form. This demonstration is essential to making the larger point that political science has a valuable role to play in research on the New Public Management.

AUSTRALIA

Michael Pusey's *Economic Rationalism in Canberra* (Pusey 1991) examines economic policy-making and public management reform under the Australian Labor governments of the 1980s. A major contention is that policies in the domains of both economic and public management derived from the same policy paradigm, known as "economic rationalism." Using survey data, the book provides empirical evidence for the claim that senior officials embraced the main tenets of economic rationalism. These shared commitments are given substantial weight in explaining the content of public sector management reforms in Australia and the ease with which they were implemented.

Pusey describes the claims of economic rationalism as follows. First, national policies aimed at improving economic performance should cascade down the policy hierarchy, that is, from macroeconomic policy, to labor market policy, and further down to education policy. Second, government policies intended to improve economic performance should be translated into conceptually similar policies intended to improve the efficiency and effectiveness of the public sector. Third, government organizations should incorporate structural elements of private sector organizations and should model their processes on best practice in the private sector (152).

Pusey analyzes in some detail the 1987 streamlining of the machinery of government, which he regards as a watershed event. Among other changes, the restructuring reduced the number of government departments and established a two-tier ministry. The previously freestanding ministerial Department of Education, for instance, was nested within the new Department for Employment, Education, and Training. The restructuring also eliminated independent statutory boards that had participated in designing education policy at the secondary and university levels. Under Pusey's analysis, these changes reflected the increasing strength of the "right-wing" element of the ruling

Labor party as it formed its third successive government. Pusey highlights the fact that the reorganization put a member of the center-left faction (the minister for education) under a member of the economic rationalist faction (the minister for employment, education, and training). Power plays aside, Pusey interprets the reorganization in terms of an extension of economic rationalist doctrines to the organizational structure of public service in Australia.[1]

The same reorganization also eliminated the Public Service Board; formal authority over much of personnel management policy moved to the Department of Finance, the central agency responsible for controlling public spending, while responsibility for labor relations between the government and public employees passed to the newly established Department of Industrial Relations. The elimination of the independent Public Service Board widened the government's managerial prerogatives. Pusey attributes the horizontal centralization of control over civil service and labor relations to economic rationalism as well.

Pusey is particularly concerned to explain how economic rationalism became so firmly accepted in Australia. He argues that senior officials shared the political outlook and policy preferences of the economic rationalists in the cabinet. Pusey also argues that the homogeneous composition of central agencies—its staff was chiefly drawn from economics or business-related professions—contributed to a strong sense of mission in central agencies, which in turn contributed to a greater degree of ideological hegemony within executive government. In sum, he argues that the three central agencies within the Australian Commonwealth executive—Prime Minister and Cabinet, Treasury, and Finance—together functioned as the linchpin of a newly ordered system of power relations within government and that this system ensured that the government's policy preferences were implemented throughout the bureaucracy.[2]

Pusey collected interview data to explore how central agencies were able to play such a key part in pushing economic rationalism across government. In essence, economic rationalists "captured" the line bureaucracies. Officials with good economic rationalist credentials tended to be promoted to key positions within line agencies, from which they were able to influence policy. Woven into this argument is the suggestion that line agencies were adapting rationally to the rise in uncertainty over the flow of resources into their organizations.

Economic Rationalism in Canberra aspires to develop "total explanations" for selected policy events by drawing on a number of different theoretical frameworks, including the analysis of organizational coherence and interorganizational networks. The book is intended neither to test theories of government or policy-making nor to develop a narrative account of public sector management reform. But it does offer insight into factors that appear to explain why the policy preferences of the economic rationalists in the cabinet were so effectively imposed throughout the executive establishment. These factors include organizational configurations within central agencies (including educational background, sense of mission, and corporate integrity) and institutional pressures that line agencies would ignore at their peril. In this work, Pusey meets a high standard for looking at the relationship between ideas and institutions in the study of public management policy-making.

Colin Campbell and John Halligan's *Political Leadership in an Age of Constraint: The Australian Experience* (1992) covers some of the same ground as Pusey's book, but differs from it in four key respects. First, Campbell and Halligan are more systematic and expansive in their selection of public management reforms, giving, for example, considerable attention to financial management reforms, program management and budgeting, and the broad-banding of the position classification system. Second, Campbell and Halligan develop a coherent narrative account of this wider range of reforms. Third, their narrative account builds on previous studies of executive leadership and institutions in similar governmental systems. Fourth, their claims about the impact of public sector management reforms are based on a wealth of interviews with senior officials in line departments as well as central agencies. For these reasons, their book is an excellent example of a narrative account of public management policy-making.

Campbell and Halligan view extensive public management reform as evidence that the Labor government of Prime Minister Bob Hawke was capable of governing effectively during a time of fiscal constraint. Public management reform enabled the government to do more than simply translate tight fiscal policy into deep cuts in public expenditure. The authors substantiate the claim that Australia developed an impressive capacity during the 1980s to evaluate major program and expenditure decisions in terms of the strategic direction set by the cabinet's dominant coalition. The authors' analysis indicates that links between overall policy strategy and expenditure planning achieved a coherent pattern of policy innovation over the better part of a "difficult decade." Campbell and Halligan also provide reasons to believe that financial management reforms improved the efficiency of large-scale production-type operations, such as revenue administration.

Campbell and Halligan pay close attention to the exercise of authority and leadership by Prime Minister Bob Hawke and Treasury Minister Paul Keating, on one hand, and to the organizational capacity of the central agencies with which they worked most closely, on the other. The central thread of their argument is that achieving a coherent policy strategy and, within this, public management policy innovation, was due to a "symbiosis" between top political executives and senior officials. This symbiosis is examined from two angles. The first analysis is in terms of intentional action: the way in which key ministers constructed and performed their roles is accorded great importance. The relationship between ministers and officials is described as "tight" in some respects and "loose" in others, in a way that produced political authoritativeness and internal policy dialogue as well as organizational commitment and follow-through. In Campbell and Halligan's book, as in Pusey's account, ministers and officials are described as having shared the policy paradigm of economic rationalism as well as having a mutual interest in being respected for managing the economy in an apparently responsible manner. The second set of factors Campbell and Halligan describe as contributing to a symbiosis between ministers and officials are institutional factors, including the composition of the Australian higher civil service, the organizational design of the center of government, and bureaucratic competence in particular agencies. Campbell and Halligan's study, which is only briefly summarized here, is a substantial contribution to the case study research literature on the New Public Management.

Spencer Zifcak's *New Managerialism: Administrative Reform in Whitehall and Canberra* (1994) includes careful case studies of three public management initiatives that took place during the 1980s: corporate planning, program management and budgeting, and financial management improvement. The author traces all three initiatives to a committee of inquiry appointed by the newly installed government of Bob Hawke and chaired by businessman John Reid. In 1983, the committee of inquiry firmly endorsed the theme of "managing for results." Specifically, the report recommended that departmental officials and ministers use corporate planning processes to agree on goals, strategies, and priorities. The report also called for a servicewide financial management improvement program to make managers more aware of the resource implications of their decisions. A working party that included private sector consultants subsequently canvased the views of senior officials in Canberra as to what management improvements were required. On the basis of these consultations, the working party recommended that corporate planning be introduced in every department to achieve a more effective fit between each agency's resource requirements and the government's policy goals. The corporate planning process—which appears to be a textbook version of strategic planning (Mintzberg 1994)—was to be driven by departments rather than ministers.

The Department of Finance allowed experience with corporate planning and program budgeting to build up quietly over a few years before publicly announcing the Financial Management Improvement Program (FMIP) in 1986. Zifcak's study suggests that the Australian reforms resulted in an impressive delegation of budgetary and financial management responsibilities. This result is attributed to the gradual emergence of a synergy between the budgetary and management frameworks. The new budget procedures gave Finance confidence that overall spending by departments was under firm control, reducing their concern as to how departments spent the funds allocated to them. Finance also introduced a comprehensive running cost system (i.e., including staff costs), under which unspent funds could be carried forward. Departments were then pressured to reduce their running costs by 1.25 percent each year. It was up to departments to decide how to produce this "efficiency dividend."

What Zifcak presents, in effect, is a list of elements necessary to decentralizing the budgetary systems of government. But his analysis also considers how management capitalized on the process. In particular, he analyzes how the relationship between Finance and various departments evolved over the reform period. While not disputing Campbell and Halligan's claim that the supply divisions within Finance were unevenly committed to changing their routines, Zifcak concludes that the "Department of Finance did withdraw to a very considerable extent from detailed intervention in departmental affairs" (118). Zifcak's chapters on Australia form an excellent study of the content and organizational politics of managerial reform in government.[3]

Anna Yeatman's article "The Concept of Public Management and the Australian State in the 1980s" (Yeatman 1987) focuses on how the culture of the Australian public service has been affected by the public sector management reforms of the 1980s. Yeatman uses sociological theory to analyze the attributes and origins of this outcome, relying heavily on Alvin Gouldner's theory of the "rise of the new class" to establish her descriptive and causal claims. The method is explicitly theoretical rather than an attempt at a "total explanation" of Australian public sector management reform.

According to sociological analysis, members of the technical intelligentsia are more likely to embrace managerialist culture than are mandarins. Yeatman's explanation of cultural change in Australia's public sector takes account of structural factors and voluntaristic action. Structural factors include the absence of an entrenched mandarinate, which opened up room for the technical intelligentsia at the top of the Australian public service. But her main argument is that the growth of the interventionist welfare state in the early 1970s provided the foundation for a new managerialist class.

According to Yeatman, the Australian public service culture became "managerialist" during the 1980s when university-educated candidates were selected for middle- and senior-level positions on the basis of merit (as opposed to seniority, for example). These types of officeholders are notable for their commitment to a highly rationalized and task-oriented conception of public administration whose generic job description is "management improvement." Entrenched ideas about the means by which goals are to be accomplished become suspect; nothing remains sacred. At the same time, such managers are "teleologically promiscuous" (349). In contrast to classical bureaucrats, idea-type managers are not committed to substantive public service obligations, such as fair and equitable government administration; nor are they committed to the substantive ends of the professions on which the welfare state has relied to pursue social goals. Such managers therefore use their technical knowledge and procedural commitments to fashion improved means to accomplish ends specified by political authorities and top officials.

Yeatman's article points out that the ranks of the trade unions were also staffed with university-trained individuals. The largest trade union came to be led by a member of the new class of technical intelligentsia: Bob Hawke. As a result, both the political executive and the upper reaches of Canberra officialdom were recruiting from the same social base, contributing to the symbiosis noted by Campbell and Halligan as well as by Pusey.

UNITED KINGDOM

Colin Campbell and Graham Wilson's *The End of Whitehall: Death of a Paradigm?* (1995) is a wide-ranging thematic and narrative account of public management policy-making in the United Kingdom under Margaret Thatcher and John Major. Campbell and Wilson argue that public sector management reform began in 1976 when the International Monetary Fund imposed stringent conditions, including a ceiling on what many departments could spend, in exchange for rescuing the pound. Hence, according to Campbell and Wilson, the practice of imposing "cash limits" on departments was well established by the time the Conservatives defeated Labour and Thatcher became prime minister. "Wilson introduced this system," the authors claim. "Callaghan extended and entrenched it. Mrs Thatcher took gratuitous credit for it" (21).

The authors view as highly significant Mrs. Thatcher's use of cash limits to restrain wages in the public sector. The government became an aggressive player in negotiations with public service unions, leading to strikes in 1980. Campbell and Wilson maintain that "the bitter 1980 negotiations with public service unions produced settlements much more consistent with cash limits than thought possible" (27). The government's stance in these negotiations appears to have been of considerable significance in controlling the growth of public expenditure.

Campbell and Wilson attribute Mrs. Thatcher's apparently pervasive influence over management reform to her overall leadership style rather than to particular interventions such as establishing the Efficiency Unit within the prime minister's office or shaping high-level civil service appointments. As a rule, the prime minister "operated largely under the assumption that matters of detail would fall into line once her government won widespread acceptance for its economic strategy" (26). Mrs. Thatcher's approach to political leadership, furthermore, was more consonant with managerialism than was that of her immediate predecessors. "Whereas the three previous governments had placed considerable emphasis on consensus coordination, focusing on policy objectives across the board, Mrs. Thatcher had stressed that ministers and departments state their objectives and concentrate their efforts on achieving these" (35). Mrs. Thatcher also held her cabinet colleagues responsible for making a mark on their departments. This stance, according to Campbell and Wilson, stemmed from a disapproval for her predecessors' leadership approach.

Nonetheless, Mrs. Thatcher's own decision agenda and prime ministerial interventions made a difference. The authors point to her creation of bits of machinery at the center of government dedicated to management improvement. The Efficiency Adviser was placed within the Prime Minister's Office, and the Efficiency Unit and the Next Steps team were set up in the Cabinet Office. In this way, the prime minister did not have to rely exclusively on the Treasury, the Civil Service Department (which she abolished in 1981), or nongovernmental bodies to devise ways to improve civil service management. The people operating within these bits of machinery were closely identified with the prime minister herself. Indeed, they seemed to have succeeded in creating a "keen awareness of the Prime Minister's backing for the government's various managerial initiatives" (65). At the same time, Mrs. Thatcher allowed the Treasury to become the main locus of responsibility at the center for governmental management. For instance, when she dismantled the Civil Service Department, most of its functions were turned back to the Treasury. Campbell and Wilson argue that Mrs. Thatcher used the Treasury reasonably effectively to pursue the broad outlines of policies she endorsed for improving public management.[4]

Campbell and Wilson also explore management reform under John Major. This period is notable for the multitude of public management improvement initiatives operating side by side and, arguably, at cross-purposes. Among the initiatives of this period were the Next Steps Initiative (established under Thatcher), the Citizens Charter Initiative, Competing for Quality (i.e., market testing), and the Private Finance Initiative. The authors seek to explain why so many different initiatives were launched as well as why pressures for coordinating them seem to have been so flaccid.

The main idea of the Citizens Charter initiative was to oblige providers of public services to define and publicize service standards, to measure their service performance, and to create channels for handling citizen complaints. By focusing on service quality rather than efficiency, the charter initiative was based on different values from those most closely associated with Major's predecessor. Indeed, the Citizens Charter, according to Campbell and Wilson, was devised as a means by which John Major could differentiate himself from Thatcherites in the run-up to the 1992 general election. The concept of the Citizens Charter was woven into a discourse that borrowed from "the continental concept of the social market." The intended message was that Major combined neo-liberalism with sensitivity to the needs of the average citizen. After the general election, the Citizens Charter was transformed from a campaign slogan into a centrally managed public management initiative closely identified with the prime minister.

After the 1992 election, Major created a ministerial portfolio of the collection of small units in the Cabinet Office dealing with public management reform and placed them under the new Office for Public Service and Science (OPSS). William Waldegrave was placed in charge of the OPSS, the first time a minister was singularly responsible for the government's handling of public sector management reform. An ambitious Thatcherite whose political standing had earlier been weakened by his performance as minister of health, Waldegrave "seized the opportunity to take the reins of the reinventing government bandwagon" (72). A specific initiative to emerge from OPSS was market testing. According to the authors, departments were forced to come up with £1.5 billion worth of business that could be given out to tender. Meanwhile, the Treasury and other government departments continued to implement the Next Steps Initiative by establishing agencies, each with tailor-made systems of personnel and financial management.

The new initiatives launched from the OPSS were perceived by agency executives to be thoroughly inconsistent with the managerialist conception of Next Steps agencies. Campbell and Wilson maintain that the Citizens Charter, and especially market testing, came to be seen as the reintroduction of micromanagement, this time from OPSS rather than from the Treasury. Many respondents feared that market testing would undermine their efforts to improve performance through better teamwork.

Campbell and Wilson identify a key respect in which officials felt disillusioned by the Next Steps Initiative. From the perspective of officials, agencies were created so that government operations could be performed in a businesslike manner within departments. But when the planned cycle of three-year reviews began, the main question the government seemed to be asking was not how much progress had been made within the Next Steps framework, but whether the agency should be privatized. The result, according to Campbell and Wilson, was profound disillusionment over the direction of management reform under John Major's government.

There are several strands to Campbell and Wilson's explanation as to why management reform under John Major's government seemed to lack consistency and continuity. First, public management reform became more politicized, particularly after the OPSS was established as a ministerial portfolio. Thatcher had exercised unusual leverage over public management, but she had largely done so by creating a "symbiosis between Whitehall managerialists and the government" (79). Second, policy entrepreneurship in the realm of management reform was unconstrained by a consistent line of public management doctrine or political discourse. Third, the authors consider John Major to have been the passive leader of a seriously fragmented administration, a pattern of executive leadership that inhibits policy coordination.

Andrew Gray and Bill Jenkins's article "The Management of Change in Whitehall: The Experience of the FMI," (1991) focuses on the Financial Management Initiative (FMI), launched in 1983. The FMI was presented as a step beyond the earlier Rayner scrutinies exercise toward improving civil service management conducted under the auspices of the Efficiency Unit. The FMI enveloped several concepts: ministers would have access to information they needed to increase the efficiency and effectiveness of their departments; cost-conscious program management would be fostered by devolving responsibility for budget execution; and organizational and program performance would be more systematically evaluated. The unifying idea of the FMI was "accountable management"—according to which formal administrative systems are used to structure responsibility, channel information flows, and enforce accountability on line managers. Gray and Jenkins trace the accountable management doctrine back to the Fulton Report issued twelve years earlier.

According to Gray and Jenkins, the FMI was not the most comprehensive approach to improving civil service management then under discussion. The authors maintain that a more comprehensive initiative encompassing human resource as well as financial management was advocated by external management consultants who, together with the Efficiency Unit, were broadly thought to have had the prime minister's ear. But Gray and Jenkins discern Treasury influence in the decision to center the reform program around managerial accounting systems and budget execution processes.

A small number of officials were appointed to champion the principles of the FMI and to guide departments' efforts to take up the initiative. Organizationally, this group came under the Financial Management Unit, itself jointly managed by the Treasury and the Civil Service Department. The FMI worked as an invitation to explore new terrain on a number of fronts without defining any particular outcome. Departments were called upon to realign organizational responsibilities, devolve responsibility for budget execution, strengthen cost accounting systems, and devise measures of operational performance.

Gray and Jenkins suggest that FMI induced change by opening a wedge within departments, through which some units could march in pursuit of larger budgets or managerial convenience. They hypothesize that units whose outputs could be calculated would be most inclined to jump on the FMI bandwagon, because in relative terms they could more easily strengthen their hand in the budget process. The authors maintain, "FMI systems have tended to be relatively coherently developed in areas of executive (i.e., operational) activity" (50).

But a number of those who had initially joined the FMI bandwagon jumped off it over the years. The authors say sources of disillusionment included missed opportunities to use the FMI as a vehicle for overall management improvement; a long delay in aggregating staff and other categories of operational expenditure into a unified running costs regime; the priority given by the Treasury to economic over efficiency objectives; a skill shortage within the civil service, specifically of accountants; and ministers' frequent disregard for the FMI philosophy.

Spencer Zifcak's *New Managerialism: Administrative Reform in Whitehall and Canberra* (1994) includes a case study of the FMI. Zifcak's thesis is that FMI was a strategy employed by officials at the center to seize some initiative in the face of the Thatcher government's initial "attacks" on the civil service; these early forays sought to reduce the ranks of civil service personnel, impose cash limits on departmental expenditure, and drive down civil service pay. At the time, the major managerial reform initiative—the Rayner scrutinies—was run from the Efficiency Unit under the aegis of a business executive who had served in the Ministry of Defence. With the FMI, Treasury and other officials sought to integrate this policy direction with managerial concepts such as performance measurement, cost consciousness, and ministerial involvement in management.

Zifcak's account indicates that managerial authority within departments was slow to be delegated downward. He argues that a prerequisite for such delegation is a running costs system that permits operational managers to alter the mix of staff and other inputs. Such a system was not established until April 1986, apparently because the government was preoccupied with thinning the ranks of civil servants and keeping spending under control. In the meantime, financial and operational managers were at a standoff:

> Until PFOs (principal finance officers) were convinced that effective financial control systems were available to operational managers and were satisfied that these systems could be utilized effectively, their natural tendency was to advise against assignment of financial responsibility. At the same time, operational managers argued that unless responsibility was assigned, they could neither obtain experience nor demonstrate their competence. This particular disagreement was never fully resolved and blighted many attempts to achieve even a modest degree of intra-departmental delegation. (56)

By the time a running costs system was introduced in 1986, interest and enthusiasm had waned, and as a strategy to achieve change, FMI was a spent force.

UNITED STATES

Donald Kettl's essay on the Clinton administration's Reinventing Government campaign, "Building Lasting Reform: Enduring Questions, Missing Answers" (1995), is an artful mixture of political analysis and commentary on a reform-in-progress. Kettl contends that the National Performance Review (NPR) is destined to become a landmark in public sector management reform in the U.S. federal government. In political terms, the NPR demonstrates that public management reform is an issue that can remain near the top of a presidential agenda for at least an entire term. In substantive terms, NPR demonstrates that executive leadership from the White House can have an impact on the management of federal departments and on specific activities or programs. In both respects, NPR seems to have broken the mold of public management reform in the federal government.

Kettl sets out to explain why the public sector management initially reached the presidential agenda in 1993. The most immediate reason was the electoral strength of H. Ross Perot, who received 19 percent of the popular vote in the 1992 presidential election. Perot was seen as the latest beneficiary of what Kettl calls the "downsizing movement" in American politics, first manifest in the 1970s property tax revolts. As deficit reduction had been among the key themes of Perot's political rhetoric, the Clinton White House concluded that it would be politically dangerous to disregard the downsizing movement. Politically, NPR was designed to garner the Perot vote in the 1996 presidential election.

The Clinton administration capitalized on popular support for downsizing by linking NPR to a dramatic cut in the civilian federal workforce, claiming budget savings of $100 million. According to Kettl, downsizing was at the core of the "high politics" of NPR, played out in relations between the presidency and Congress. The administration put itself on the hook to achieve personnel reductions and cost savings.

Doctrinally, NPR took on board many of the "principles" of effective public management advocated by David Osborne and Ted Gaebler in *Reinventing Government*, a book that became a best-seller during the 1992 presidential campaign. The sources of these principles included doctrines of total quality management, reengineering, and organizational culture. Employee empowerment and customer service emerged as vital themes, sitting uncomfortably with downsizing. Substantively, NPR encompassed changes to the federal procurement system, the devolution of responsibility for certain areas of personnel management (e.g., recruiting), implementation of the Government Performance and Results Act of 1993, reorganization of the Office for Management and Budget, a program to establish service standards, and a wide array of measures that were closely linked to specific departments and agencies. The whole pattern of activity and ideas tended to support the administration's claim that NPR's aim was to make the federal government "work better" as well as "cost less."

Kettl identifies three reasons why public sector management reform remained high on Clinton's agenda throughout his first term. First, the issue worked in Clinton's favor, evidenced by an eighteen-point jump in the president's approval rating on the heels of NPR's launch in September 1993—the largest gain Clinton experienced in his first term. Second, after the Republican sweep of Congress in the 1994 election, public sector management reform looked to be one of few areas in which the administration could break the policy gridlock. Third, NPR came to be identified with Vice President Al Gore, who saw substantial benefit in being regarded as a leader in this area. All in all, "NPR quickly became part of the foundation for the president's 1996 reelection campaign" (11).

Kettl notes that earlier attempts at public management reform in the United States failed to get as far as NPR. The reorganization of the executive branch of government proposed by President Roosevelt in 1938 was voted down by a Congress that saw in the move an unfavorable shift in power to the president. But as Kettl points out, NPR was seen as a downsizing maneuver, not a plan to alter the balance of power between the president and Congress. Even the "works better" theme did not raise Congressional suspicions of executive encroachment. NPR aimed to empower line agency personnel working under political appointees. With two short-lived exceptions, NPR studiously avoided any suggestion of major reorganizations to federal departments and agencies. In the past, such proposed reorganizations met with Congressional opposition because they threatened to redraw House and Senate committee jurisdictions.

Kettl also identifies a number of ways in which the political success of NPR was due to more than just the popular appeal of downsizing the federal government. First, the administration did not create a new bureaucracy to run NPR. The "reinventing government" effort was organized as a project in the vice president's office, staffed mainly by career officials on loan from their home agencies. Second, the administration was skillful in its use of the media to define the issue of public management reform. An oft-cited example is a late-night appearance by Vice President Al

Gore on a television talk show during which he used a hammer to smash an ashtray in an attempt to criticize federal procurement practices. Third, the administration headed off opposition to downsizing from labor union leaders representing organized federal employees. The fact that unions supported NPR is mainly attributed to the administration's willingness to make structural and informal changes to labor-management relations within the federal government. A National Partnership Council composed of top union leaders and selected cabinet members was established, one of whose tasks was to assist the administration in proposing new legislation concerned with labor-management relations. Kettl notes that there may have been a political as well as a managerial logic to finding over half of redundancies from the ranks of middle managers, when unions tended to represent nonsupervisory workers. Fourth, the administration won the support of political appointees and career officials for NPR by marketing it as a means to improve management.

However, from the perspective of the Clinton administration, NPR was not, in fact, an unqualified political success. As Kettl puts it, "Congress proved eager to support the savings proposals in general but often backed away from taking particular actions required to achieve them." Several of the budget-cutting proposals, such as closing the military's in-house medical school, were quietly rejected by the relevant powers in Congress. The legislative branch also blocked plans to trim staffing levels in the Treasury Department's enforcement activities. And the legislative process associated with public management reform was fraught with conflict.

Kettl credits NPR with speeding up managerial improvement in the federal government, especially where cabinet and career officials "seized the reins"; consummated political agreements with legislative overseers; lobbied for the elimination of OMB clearances; worked to change the culture of bureaucracy; and supported proposals from the lower ranks. To some degree, the reinvention movement achieved concrete legislative results, especially in terms of streamlining the procurement process.

Yet Kettl's main contention is that the reinvention process is not self-sustaining:

> Doubts remain about the extent to which the reorganized Office of Management and Budget will be able to implement the Government Performance and Results Act, and contradictions in the "works better" and "costs less" formula are bound to bear some bitter fruit.

CANADA

The principal work on public management reform in Canada is Peter Aucoin's *The New Public Management: Canada in Comparative Perspective* (1995). Aucoin's main empirical interest is to describe and evaluate Canadian public management policies rather than to account for them. Aucoin maintains that the Canadian federal government has done relatively little to increase accountability for outputs and outcomes; spending cutbacks have not been accompanied by creative strategies to improve efficiency; and administrative decentralization is stuck at the departmental level. Canada, he argued at the time, lagged considerably behind its fellow Westminster systems.

The Canadian case of public management reform in the 1980s, however, does not lack for policy events. In 1986, Brian

Mulroney's government formally endorsed a program known as Increased Ministerial Authority and Accountability (IMAA). IMAA established a process whereby central agencies and departments could see a reduction in some central administrative controls in return for strengthening results-oriented accountability (129). In 1989, the prime minister gave his support to a "major internal assessment and renewal" of public management, called Public Service 2000. At about the same time, the principal central agency—the Treasury Board Secretariat—approved five Special Operating Agencies (SOAs), whose structures and procedures were to be reorganized along business lines.

Aucoin contends that these policy initiatives made no more than a modest dent in the practice of public management in the federal government. Even after four years, IMAA was implemented in at most a third of government departments. The concept of SOAs, though applied in such areas as common service provision, did not emerge as the typical organizational form for operational activities within line departments. The implementation of both initiatives disappointed those who had hoped for a large-scale transformation of the Canadian federal government.

Aucoin attributes a failure to push these initiatives further at the implementation stage to the absence of solid and persistent ministerial support: cabinet ministers in Brian Mulroney's government simply did not much care about public management reform. This explanation comprises two main threads. First, Mulroney's style of political leadership involved continually brokering deals with various geographic and other interests. While the prime minister occasionally engaged with public management issues, his attention to them was never sustained.[5] In Aucoin's words, "management reform was essentially an internal bureaucratic preoccupation that could be tolerated so long as it did not detract from (the) political agenda" (15). Second, cabinet ministers were not receptive to emerging doctrines of New Public Management. In particular, they did not set much store by the view that increased efficiency and effectiveness require extensive administrative decentralization. The government continued to hold the view that efficiencies could be achieved by cutting overhead line items and by undertaking ministerial-level reviews of all government programs.

Despite ministerial indifference to public management reform, significant changes did occur in financial management, service delivery, and the provision of common services. Changes in financial management included the establishment of a running costs regime; that is, departments were granted the authority to move funds among running cost accounts, and controls were removed on staffing levels. Aucoin suggests that these changes were promoted in the main by the career civil service, whose leaders were receptive to claims that administrative centralization handicapped the performance of government departments. Improved service delivery was achieved across a wide variety of operations in Canada and, as Aucoin points out, without the aid of a government-wide policy of setting service standards and measuring performance. Instead, the driving force was the attitude of operational managers and staff. These attitudes were given some cultural validation within the Canadian public service, especially through the Public Service 2000 initiative, which explicitly propounded the view that government should seek to satisfy citizens as customers (199).

Common services provision was reorganized along business lines, while departments were given considerable discretion over their choice of supplier.[6] These changes reflected the influence of marketization ideas within the federal public service. On the other hand, extremely limited progress has been made in personnel administration within the Canadian public service. Although a concept of strengthened managerial prerogatives was built into legislative reforms, Aucoin maintains that union objections have made managers wary of exercising their greater prerogatives.[7]

By the early 1990s, the fragmentation of Canada's executive arm of government also came to be seen as a problem (199). In an attempt to represent a range of geographical and sectoral interests in the executive, the cabinet had nearly forty members. But by the early 1990s, such representation was considered to undermine the government's ability to pursue a coherent policy agenda. An official review of cabinet structure was begun in 1992. When Kim Campbell became prime minister in 1993, she carried those recommendations further, reducing the number of departments from thirty-two to twenty-three. This streamlined structure was adopted by the Liberal government of Jean Chrétien, which came to power later in the same year. Following the moves to consolidate the structure of government, public management reform in Canada came to be focused on merging organizations and downsizing staff. As Aucoin observes:

> The consolidated portfolio and departmental structures, especially when combined with the Liberal government's new Expenditure Management System, may well provide an organizational and decision-making framework within which increased deregulation of central agency controls and enhanced delegation of authority are more probable. (133)

SWEDEN

The literature on public sector management reform in Sweden does not include a book-length study in English. But two general articles, by Rune Premfors (1991) and Jon Pierre (1993), and a book chapter by Stuart Wilks (1996) provide significant and valuable insight into the case. These three pieces will be considered together in this section.

Premfors maintains that an extended and comprehensive period of public sector management reform began with the Social Democrats' return to power in late 1982, after six years in opposition. According to Premfors, the previous three-party coalition pursued reform in an "ad hoc" manner. The Social Democrats, on the other hand, began by establishing a ministry for public administration, the Civildepartment, led initially by a well-known proponent of decentralization in the public sector, Bo Holmberg. Premfors describes the minister and officials as enjoying considerable latitude in formulating the government's approach to public sector management and proposing policy measures.

Under Pierre's analysis, the key issue around which reform of the Swedish public sector revolved was how to shore up the legitimacy of a system of public policy and finance that delivered adequate public services, but at the cost of heavy taxation. Cracks in the system's perceived legitimacy first appeared in 1976, when the Social Democrats lost power for the first time in forty years to a nonsocialist opposition that sought to embarrass the SAP (Social Democratic) government by associating red tape with the whole notion of the welfare state and redistributive politics. This rhetorical strategy worked, creating an outlet for citizen frustration with bureaucratic red tape.

Back in power in the early 1980s, the Social Democrats were publicly committed to keeping the public sector from expanding in relation to the economy as a whole (Premfors 1991, 86). An approach to public service reform, rooted in critiques of the Swedish model emanating from the Social Democratic Left, was put forward by the Civildepartment, a central agency. The main thrust of the proposal was to revamp the Swedish model to allow for greater decentralization and citizen participation in public service delivery. In the language of the 1980s, the goal was to practice a "client-oriented model" of state-citizen relations. Premfors adds that the Social Democrats perceived decentralization to be conducive to reinforcing political control and reinvigorating party life (Premfors 1991, 92).

Within the government, opinion was divided as to how to deal with the legitimacy problems of the Swedish model of the public sector. Cobbling together a coalition of support sufficient to carry through any particular policy proposal was always a difficult task.[8] In addition, the history of public administration in Sweden provided no predefined role for the Civildepartment. Traditionally in Sweden, government had limited involvement with the organizations that delivered public services. This convention was reinforced by a centuries-old constitutional provision establishing the state administration's executive agencies as autonomous from the ministries to which they were attached. Any attempt to exercise policy influence over administrative decisions cut against the grain of institutional relationships in Swedish public administration.

The Civildepartment tackled these constraints in two ways. The first was in its use of rhetoric. Under Bo Holmberg, the Civildepartment was notable for its promotion of an "enterprise" and "service" culture in the context of an overall program of "renewal" for the public sector. Second, this central agency focused on drawing up proposed legislation that agencies would have a statutory mandate to apply. Holmberg managed to shepherd through Parliament a bill that created a process for deregulating national programs delivered by local government. Under the bill, known as the "Free Commune Experiment," a few municipalities and counties had the right to apply for exemption from selected national laws or regulations for a limited period of time, and the Civildepartment was to represent the state in the process of implementing the legislation. Pierre considers the Free Commune Experiment a relative success in deregulating local government, contributing to decentralization on a wide scale. Municipalities and counties implementing national programs had greater responsibilities and latitude of operation in the early 1990s than they had had in the early 1980s.

In Sweden, planning and budgeting procedures were then revised over a ten-year period, establishing a type of corporate management process. Ministries began to issue "planning directives" to the executive agencies located within their jurisdiction, and executive agencies became obliged to submit to the government detailed objectives along with their budget submissions. Wilks maintains that "the establishment of goals and objectives takes place as an integral part of the budget process and through dialog between the government, the ministries, and the agencies" (Wilks 1996, 26). The implication here is that government is making unconventional use of the budget process to steer the executive agencies. Wilks gives the new budget system credit for significantly increasing the availability and importance of cost information. But he endorses the claim that "the objectives are often too vague, the methods of evaluation ill-developed, and the suitability of management by objectives to the Swedish political culture is often questionable."

Following the rejection of solidaristic, economy-wide wage policies in the 1960s and 1980s, the system of pay in the Swedish public sector appears also to have been fundamentally altered. During much of the 1980s, the centralized system of determining pay was gradually eroded, and it was replaced in 1991 with a more flexible and individualized system. Wilks states that "this new system is now in full operation and the extent to which pay bargaining has been decentralized should not be underestimated" (Wilks 1996, 34).

There were several serious difficulties faced by the Social Democrats in tackling the weakening legitimacy of the "Swedish model" and charting a course forward. But the literature reviewed here suggests that policies aimed at reforming public sector management have succeeded in seeing off opposition challenges as well as stemming any powerful groundswell for privatization.

GERMANY

Like in Sweden, relatively little has been written in English on public sector management reform in Germany. A considerable literature on the overall development of the German state exists in English. But—unlike Sweden—there has been a relative absence of policy events in public sector management reform to be explained in Germany. According to Arthur Benz and Klaus Goetz (1996), "continuity and stability were the hallmarks of public-sector development in the 1980s" (6). More or less the same characterization applies to the first half of the 1990s. The main task in analyzing the German case is therefore to explain continuity and stability.

Benz and Goetz contend that proposals to alter Germany's formal institutional arrangements in the German public sector are easily vetoed: "institutional change tends to require the need to go through formal procedures, a process which encourages participation and open confrontation of conflicting interests and thus works against swift, single-handed institutional reorganization" (16). This observation applies to the federal system as a whole as well as to the departmental level within the federal government. A second explanation for institutional continuity and stability in Germany is weak pressures for change. Benz and Goetz suggest that a key reason for the lack of demand for change is the fact that the normative basis of state activity has remained stable. Specifically, broad support for the welfare state has been sustained. The authors also stress that many state-sponsored activities are carried out by nondepartmental and private-law organizations, a pattern that became still more pronounced over the 1980s and 1990s. Benz and Goetz maintain that this pattern explains why there is widespread support for the existing style of state-society relations and resistance to their major reorientation according to market ideologies.

The main point of qualification attached to this line of argument is that new ideas have been implemented in a pragmatic fashion (20). Implementing ideas in a pragmatic fashion means exploiting opportunities to modify procedures and informal ways of working while leaving formal institutional arrangements intact. The new ideas have generally referred to policies and programs rather than to management. The more general point is that changes in public management occur in Germany by developing and implementing programmatic policies.

Hans-Ulrich Derlien in "Patterns of Postwar Administrative Development in Germany" (1996) reinforces the impression that issues surrounding public management are normally taken up in the context of revamping specific public policies. According to Derlien's analysis, public management rarely emerges as an issue in its own right because the German public sector lacks a focal point for promoting administrative change, which is in turn, in part, because "a fully-fledged civil service ministry or interdepartmental personnel commissions are alien to the German system" (33).

Although Benz and Goetz mention that partial reorganizations along business lines have taken place at the municipal level in Germany, Derlien provides a more elaborate discussion:

> The imperative to contain public expenditures . . . was a permanent feature of the period from the mid-1970s to the mid-1980s, reinforced by the political rhetoric of the time, and has become even more visible as a consequence of the heavy financial burdens that unification has entailed. In particular, local government has appeared to be more innovative in responding to scarcity, owing to the vulnerability of its revenue base and the ever-increasing financial burdens imposed by Federal cutbacks. Thus, it is small wonder that local government was the first to jump on the new managerialist bandwagon, stressing the service function of local government in rhetoric and reinforcing cost accounting and the controller concept in practice. (40–41)

Some recent unpublished writings on public management in Germany also call attention to changing doctrines and practices at the municipal level (Löffler 1996). The most prominent doctrinal package is the New Steering Model. The ideas are exemplified by the organization and management of the Dutch city of Tilburg, which has served as an instance of "best practice." According to Helmut Klages and Elke Löffler:

> The New Steering Model was marketed extensively by the Municipal Association for Administrative Rationalization among its local government members. Meanwhile the New Steering Model has advanced to the almost exclusive model of internal modernization of German local governments. In 1996, half the municipalities with more than 5000 inhabitants were trying to put some element of the New Steering Model into practice. (Klages and Löffler 1996, 5)

The image we might derive from this account is that public management reform in Germany is a bottom-up process. Certainly, the pressure for reform is felt most at the municipal level, and a kind of "movement" to change municipal public management is afoot.[9] Sounding a cautionary note, however, Klages and Löffler state that "there are not enough indications yet whether the modernization process will eventually move upwards" (1).

FROM SINGLE CASE TO COMPARATIVE RESEARCH

Is there a comparative research enterprise lurking within what is manifestly an idiographic research style? And, if so, should that latent comparative research enterprise be systematically pursued? My judgment is that the answer to the first question is yes; to the second question, no—at least at this point in the development of the research literature.

I believe, although I risk overgeneralizing, that the narrative case studies are concerned with how much change in the structure and operation of executive government occurred between the end of the 1970s and the time of writing. This question was clearly on the minds of Campbell and Wilson (1995) in their study of the United Kingdom, *The End of Whitehall*, for instance. Similarly, Zifcak determined that somewhat more change in financial management practices occurred in Australia as compared to Britain. Derlien, writing on Germany, concludes that change at the federal level has been modest during the 1980s and 1990s, though not negligible over a longer span of time. As illustrated by these works, systemic organizational change is a case outcome of common interest: a main research issue is why so much, or so little, changes.

The focus on systemic organizational change is natural for scholars who identify with the field of public administration (PA). First, PA views organizational structures and processes as having significant consequences for the performance of the executive function in government (Lynn 1996). Events that change organizational structures and processes across executive government therefore naturally draw attention. Second, systemic organizational change in executive government is currently a subject of policy dialogue. The tone of discussion about NPM suggests that systemic organizational change in executive government is desirable. Addressing the subject of systemic organizational change is wholly appropriate for PA scholars.[10]

If systemic organizational change in executive government is a standard case outcome, then perhaps the field is poised to become a mature area of comparative public policy research. Behind this conjecture is Przeworski's (1987) observation that fields of comparative public policy take off when they "catch a dependent variable." The problem, however, is that systemic organizational change is not defined in a standard way. Hood (1996), for example, substantiates the argument that a great deal of administrative change has occurred in the United Kingdom by discussing industrial privatization under the Conservative government. Even when NPM is defined in terms of changes in the core public sector, variety in the definition of systemic organizational change is to be expected, since the concept of "organization" is itself highly contested (Morgan 1983). Classical organization theory entails a view of systemic organizational change as occurring when formal reorganizations take place and new administrative systems are implanted. Socio-technical theories entail a view of systemic organizational change as a matrix of changes in the design of tasks, physical and informational flows, and informal social relations among role occupants (Leonard-Barton 1995). Economic theories consider systemic organizational change to be a material change in the incentives facing individuals throughout the organization (Milgrom and Roberts 1992). Cultural theories consider systemic change to have occurred when belief systems and patterns of social relations are altered in organizations (Douglas 1990). The meaning of systemic organization change thus depends heavily on the theoretical frame of reference.

The link between theoretical commitments and definitions of systemic organizational change is illustrated by Aucoin's *The*

New Public Management: Canada in Comparative Perspective (1995). Aucoin brands Canada as a "laggard" among the Westminster systems. The main reason is that New Zealand and the United Kingdom reorganized their government departments to separate policy from operational responsibilities, whereas Canada has not. The claim that Canada is a laggard overlooks the fact that service delivery systems and organizational cultures were substantially changed during the 1980s as a result of the quality management movement. Aucoin's judgment about how much systemic organizational change has taken place in Canada is seemingly due to an unstated theoretical commitment to classical organization theory, as against socio-technical or cultural theories.

It seems unlikely that scholars will converge on a common definition of systemic organizational change in government and thereby "catch a dependent variable." For purposes of understanding the politics of public management policy, an alternative approach should therefore be considered. One such approach is to focus on explaining *policy choices*. Concrete examples of policy choices include machinery of government changes in Australia, the United Kingdom's shift to cash limits on departmental spending, the adoption of output-budgeting in New Zealand, Canada's policy to marketize common services, and Sweden's shift to agency-level collective bargaining. A research program focused on policy choices is much less likely to founder on the lack of a common definition of the dependent variable or case outcome than will research explaining systemic organizational change.[11]

For the literature on public management policy-making to progress rapidly, a radical conservative approach is needed:

radical in the sense of departing from what has become the focus of research efforts; conservative in the sense of adopting a standard disciplinary regimen for the study of public policy-making. This radical-conservative approach is pursued in the following chapter.

CHAPTER THREE

Comparative Analysis of Public Management Policy-Making

This chapter aims to demonstrate that research on public management policy could quickly advance if scholars were to converge on a similar research design—specifically, in the definition of case outcomes, selection of explanatory frameworks, and use of comparative methods. The first research task undertaken here is to explain public management policy change in three cases that exemplify the New Public Management: the United Kingdom, Australia, and New Zealand. The second research task is to bring the comparative method to bear in explaining similarities and differences between these "benchmark cases," taken as a group, and three other cases: Sweden, the United States, and Germany.

Public management policy refers to government-wide institutional rules in the areas of expenditure planning and financial management, civil service and labor relations, procurement, organization and methods, and audit and evaluation. In the benchmark cases of NPM, comprehensive change in public management policy occurred; that is to say, change in public management policy occurred in each of the areas just enumerated. For example, in the United Kingdom, changes in methods and procurement were prescribed by the Rayner scrutinies; the Financial Management Initiative prescribed changes in expenditure planning and financial management; changes in audit and evaluation were prescribed by the act establishing the National Audit Office; the Next Steps Initiative prescribed changes in organization, civil service, and financial management; the Citizens Charter Initiative prescribed changes in methods, audit, and evaluation; changes in procurement were prescribed by the Competing for Quality initiative; and the Resource Accounting and Budgeting initiative again prescribed changes in expenditure planning and financial management. The first task, then, is to provide an explanation of the similar case outcome in the benchmark cases.[1]

Once comprehensive public management policy change in the benchmark cases is explained, attention turns to the second research task. The case outcome in Sweden's central government and the U.S. federal government is similar compared to the benchmark cases of the United Kingdom, Australia, and New Zealand; however, the case outcome in Germany's federal government is substantially different compared to the benchmark cases. Explaining these similarities and differences yields generalizations about the New Public Management.

Apart from providing generalizations based on these comparisons, this chapter offers a template for further explanatory research on public management policy (see figure 2). The research goal is to understand change in public management policy using a case-oriented research style. The designated research objective is to develop limited historical generalizations, highlighting the

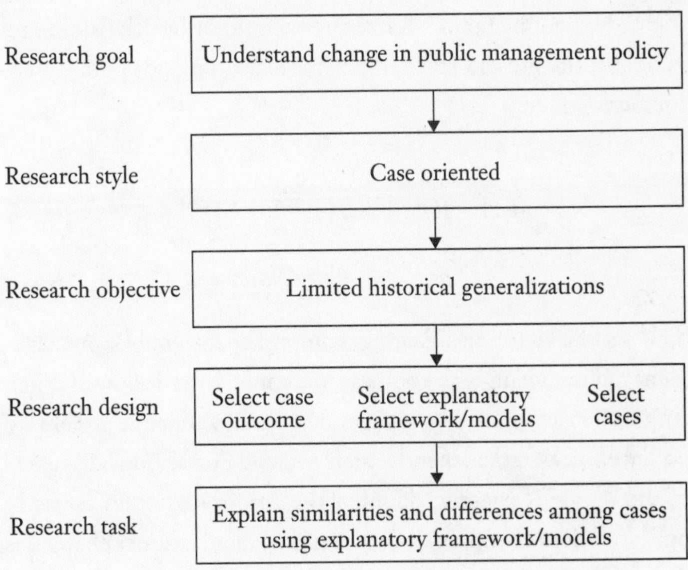

Figure 2. Comparative Research on Public Management Policy

contribution that comparative case-oriented research can make to understanding public management policy change.[2] This approach is compatible with historical institutionalism, a major research tradition in political science (Steinmo, Thelen, and Longstreth 1992).[3] Within historical institutionalism, scholars enjoy considerable discretion as to how they select and analyze cases, provided they address the tradition's characteristic analytic themes (Thelen and Steinmo 1992); among these themes is policy change within broadly stable institutions. A common research strategy for developing generalizations related to this theme is to use the comparative case study method to identify and explain differences in national policies in a particular domain, such as economic policy (Katzenstein 1978) or health (Immergut 1992). In the present study, the particular domain is public management policy.

THE RESEARCH DESIGN

Defining the Case Outcome

The rationale for designating comprehensive public management policy change as the case outcome is as follows.[4] First, comprehensive public management policy change refers to policy choices rather than to their effects. For reasons discussed in the previous chapter, defining the case outcome in terms of policy choices, as opposed to systemic organizational change, is more likely to lead diverse researchers to catch the same "dependent variable" (Przeworski 1987) and thereby accelerate research progress. Second, this definition is meaningful in terms of academic and professional discourse about the New Public Management. Saying that a country is a good example of the New Public Management is usually to indicate that substantial change in public management has occurred. The related concept of comprehensive public management policy change is more precise in its definition of *substantial* and *public management* in order to anchor the explanatory effort. Third, this definition of the case outcome is coherent with the view that the United Kingdom, Australia, and New Zealand are equally good examples of NPM (Aucoin 1995). Since all three cases are instances of comprehensive public management policy change, this view can be accepted without impinging on research progress. Thus, the designation of the case outcome makes sense given the research goal, previous discourse about NPM, and the need to "catch a dependent variable."

Case Selection

The fact that the United Kingdom, Australia, and New Zealand are considered benchmark cases of NPM is a reason to begin the research effort by focusing on them. However, achieving the research goal requires analysis of other cases as well. The case of Germany is useful analytically because comprehensive public management policy change did not occur in the 1980s and 1990s. This difference compared to the benchmark cases presents an opportunity to follow a variation-finding approach to comparative case analysis (Tilly 1984). The question is, what explains why comprehensive public management policy change occurred in the benchmark cases but not in Germany? Comparing the cases of Sweden and the United States to the benchmark cases is less advantageous from a theoretical standpoint, since they are all instances of substantial public management policy change. Analytic interest in them derives from the fact that they are different institutionally from the benchmark cases.

For purposes of comparison, the three benchmark cases can usefully be treated as a single, composite case. Analyzing composite cases is common in some areas of policy research: in the field of international development, for instance, the East Asian model of export-led growth (Wade 1990) and the Southern Cone model of economic stabilization (Foxley 1981) are both composite cases developed to facilitate argumentation about policy questions. The way Aucoin (1995) discusses NPM is similar in spirit: to address questions about public management policy, he uses the term NPM to refer to the cases of the United Kingdom, Australia, and New Zealand as a group. In this chapter, the main thrust of examining each of these cases is therefore to develop a construct referred to as the Benchmark Case. As with the East Asian and Southern Cone "cases," the justification for constructing the Benchmark Case is to advance policy research. The utility of this construct is demonstrated later in the chapter, when the Benchmark Case is compared with Sweden, the United States, and Germany.

Explanatory Framework

The chosen explanatory framework relies primarily on processual models of decision making.[5] These models explain policy change by focusing on factors that interact through time to shape the choices faced by decision makers. The explanatory framework used here incorporates three models of this type: namely, those of Kingdon (1984), Baumgartner and Jones (1993), and Levitt and March (1990). The first two are specifically concerned with public policy-making, whereas the third analyzes the process of organizational learning. Before applying these models, it is useful to describe them in general terms.

By the standards of historical institutionalism, Kingdon's explanatory framework is a highly codified manual for using "narrative methods" (Abbott 1992; Kiser 1996) to account for discrete policy changes, such as the passage of legislation.[6] Its focus is not on the process of legislative enactment, but rather on the "pre-decisional phase" of policy-making. This phase determines what policy problems gain access to the decisional agendas of elected officials, as well as what solutions or policy alternatives those officials consider. Two processes operate during this phase: agenda setting and alternative specification. Agenda setting determines which issues or problems are dealt with by decision makers; alternative specification determines which solutions they consider when a decision is to be made. These parallel processes are influenced by many factors, including the national mood, party competition, media coverage of public concerns, policy research, interest group activity, changing institutional jurisdictions, and turnover of elected and appointed officials. The coevolution of these factors shapes elected officials' beliefs and opportunities as the policy-making process moves into its decisional phase.

Kingdon places these diverse factors into three groups, called "streams." The factors are grouped in such a way that each stream influences policy-making in an analytically distinct way. The "problem stream" refers to factors that shape opinion about policy problems, including media coverage of public or elite concerns, trends in statistical indicators, and attention-grabbing events. The "policy stream" refers to factors affecting policy ideas and the crafting of specific policy alternatives. The "political stream" refers to factors—including national mood, party competition, and electoral outcomes—that influence whether elected officials are inclined to address particular policy problems or promote certain policy alternatives.

Kingdon models the temporal structure of the predecisional phase in terms of the normal career progression of a policy issue. A typical issue begins life as a matter of diffuse public concern, referred to as an item on the "systemic agenda." When it becomes a matter of concern for policy-makers, the issue is an item on the "governmental policy agenda." Once the issue is ready for resolution by policy-makers, it has arrived on their "decisional agenda." To advance from the systemic to the governmental policy agenda, an issue needs to acquire a clear definition and sense of urgency. This progression, according to Kingdon, usually occurs as the result of focusing events, such as natural disasters, epidemics, riots, or major accidents of public transport. An issue's subsequent progression from the governmental policy agenda to the decisional agenda normally occurs when the problem, policy, and political streams converge. Kingdon describes this scenario as the opening of a "window of opportunity" for policy change. This characterization echoes the well-known "garbage can model" of collective choice (Cohen, March, and Olsen 1972). In Kingdon's model, policy change happens when the policy stream (which corresponds to "solutions" in the garbage can model) becomes linked to both the problem and the political streams. Under these conditions, policy-makers are motivated to respond to policy problems by choosing a policy alternative, and policy ideas that may have lingered in the policy stream become considered by decision makers as policy proposals. Whether such conditions obtain depends on how the varied coevolving factors in the three streams come to be configured at a particular time.

In Kingdon's view, policy entrepreneurs exercise a certain degree of influence over the problem and policy streams. He discusses how policy entrepreneurs affect "the face of the issue" (Allison 1971) through timely statements and actions in the wake of a focusing event. His cases also illustrate how policy entrepreneurs promote the understanding and acceptance of policy ideas and alternatives.[7] The concept of entrepreneurship is drawn from economic theory (Knight 1921; Schumpeter 1934). In that context, performance of the entrepreneurial function brings about economic change; in Kingdon's book, performance of the entrepreneurial function brings about policy change. Any action that increases the potential for policy change is, by this definition, an act of policy entrepreneurship, and the author of such actions is a policy entrepreneur.[8]

The desires and beliefs of policy entrepreneurs are part of the explanation for policy change, but so are factors affecting the opportunities open to them. The desires and beliefs of policy entrepreneurs are exogenously determined; however, their opportunities are explained by the model. These opportunities are structured not only by formal institutional prerogatives and informal power but also by emergent phenomena such as focusing events, the national mood, and electoral outcomes. All told, Kingdon's model of policy-making allows for the influence of both human intentions and impersonal forces.[9]

A second useful model of policy change is provided by Baumgartner and Jones (1993). Their model is designed to account for major shifts in the direction of policy rather than discrete policy choices. They argue that the potential for major changes in policy direction is slight so long as decisions continue to be made within a stable policy subsystem. A subsystem is a definable institutional structure responsible for policy-making, together with formal arrangements and informal relations that influence participation in the venues where decisions are made (Baumgartner and Jones 1993, 7).[10] Their model of policy change therefore analyzes the process through which policy subsystems are undermined. This process is referred to as agenda setting. Baumgartner and Jones's model of agenda setting overlaps with Kingdon's; however, the former focuses on the process of conflict expansion through which change agents mobilize actors outside the extant policy subsystem (Schattschneider 1960). The process of mobilization operates by challenging issue images, reorganizing beliefs about issue interrelatedness (usually leading to more encompassing policy domains), and discrediting the existing institutional arrangements through which policy is routinely made. This process could prompt elected officials to disrupt the status quo, typically giving rise to a different issue image, a reordered policy domain, and a restructured policy subsystem. The basis is then laid for a change in the direction of policy.[11]

Baumgartner and Jones introduce two further concepts that are especially useful in describing the process of policy change: disequilibrium and partial equilibrium. A disequilibrium situation occurs when the potential for change in the direction of policy is high. A partial equilibrium situation occurs when the potential for directional change in policy is low. In Baumgartner and Jones's discussion, a scenario of major policy change is one where a disequilibrium situation, which changes policy direction, is followed by a partial equilibrium in which a flow of decisions consistent with that direction takes place.[12]

A third model of interest is provided by Levitt and March (1990). Their model, which is concerned with organizational learning, is useful in analyzing both stability and change in the time path of decisions. When its aspirations are not met, an organization searches for routines whose anticipated effects would satisfy them. The search process involves direct learning, that is, looking to the organization's own experience, and vicarious learning, that is, looking to the experience of other organizations. Either type of learning yields inferences about the potential effects of routines on outcomes. These inferences form the basis of ideas for changing organizational routines. The desire to satisfy aspirations leads the organization to take actions intended to change its routines. If the organization remains dissatisfied, in other words, if aspirations are unmet, the organizational learning process continues. This model helps explain why organizations change their routines even when they do not face a crisis.

The explanatory framework used to analyze the cases in this chapter draws on all three processual models just discussed (see box 1). The Kingdon model is particularly useful for its concepts of political, problem, and policy streams as well as issue career progression, policy entrepreneurship, and policy spillover effects. His model provides the basis for a theoretically informed narrative explanation of policy choices. Baumgartner and Jones's concept of partial equilibrium is useful, since comprehensive public management policy change is normally the result of a flow of decisions rather than a discrete event. This concept also points out three interlocking factors that affect public management policy choices: the policy subsystem, domain structure, and issue image. The policy subsystem refers to the institutional venues where policy-making activity occurs, such as central agencies, and to those who routinely participate in them. Domain structure refers to the conceptual organization of public policy-

Box 1. Elements of the Explanatory Framework

A. Kingdon's model

A1. Political Stream
A2. Problem Stream
A3. Policy Stream
A4. Policy Choices

B. Baumgartner and Jones's model

B1. Policy Subsystem
B2. Domain Structure
B3. Issue Image

C. Levitt and March's model

C1. Aspiration Levels
C2. Satisfaction Levels
C3. Search Process
C4. Actions
C5. Outcomes

making, which reflects beliefs about the interrelatedness of various policies.[13] A unified public management policy domain exists when policy-makers believe that institutional rules in the areas of expenditure planning and financial management, civil service and labor relations, procurement, organization and methods, and audit and evaluation are significantly interrelated. Issue image refers to the face of the issue or the dominant conception of the policy problem.[14] As we will see from the case analysis, comprehensive public management policy change can be attributed in part to change in these interlocking factors.

While Baumgartner and Jones's model explains the direction of policy-making, the specific scenario of conflict expansion, borrowed from Schattschneider, is of relatively little use in explaining the dynamics of agenda setting in the cases examined in this chapter. Kingdon's more open-ended model is better suited to these circumstances. A second limitation of Baumgartner and Jones's model is insufficient explanation as to why alternatives are considered and decisions made in a partial equilibrium situation. In the explanatory framework, this role is played by Levitt and March's model of organizational learning: the processes of direct and vicarious learning provide a flow of ideas for actions that promise to improve routines.

The research design has just been described in some detail. The task now is to explain why comprehensive public management policy change occurred in the United Kingdom, Australia, and New Zealand. The first section of the explanatory discussion provides a stylized account of conditions prior to the process of agenda setting and alternative generation in the composite Benchmark Case before it goes on to analyze the early stages of the reform process in each case. The second section analyzes later stages of the process. Taken together, the two sections provide a theoretically structured narrative explanation of the Benchmark Case.[15]

THE BENCHMARK CASES: INITIAL CONDITIONS AND THE EARLY REFORM PHASE

Public management policy-making pre-1980 fits the description of a partial equilibrium, largely confined to the specialized institutional venues of central coordinating agencies. Conflict over public management policy was normally resolved without recourse to general purpose institutional venues, such as cabinets, whose agendas were crowded with policy issues such as the macroeconomy, social welfare, and defense. Central agencies looked to their own experience as a basis for organizational learning. Existing institutional rules and routines were believed to embody experience-based knowledge about how to achieve the goals of efficiency, fairness, and accountability in a governmental context, and those who would argue for departing from established practice had to overcome daunting burdens of proof.[16] Such high burdens of proof bounded the learning path. Under these conditions, major changes in public management policy were not to be expected.

Public management policy-making pre-1980 was also internally fragmented, both conceptually and institutionally. Decisions in this domain were believed to require the application of specialized knowledge about the government's institutional rules and routines, expertise that was organized around specific administrative functions, such as budgeting, personnel administration, procurement, and auditing. Organizationally, responsibility for public management policy was divided among central agencies, which tended to specialize by groupings of administrative functions. In sum, public management was far from a unified policy domain.

The following subsections seek to identify and explain important policy events occurring during the early stages of each benchmark case. Since these events affected the policy-making process at later stages, these discussions are part of the explanation of the case outcome. The first case to be discussed is the United Kingdom. Australia and New Zealand then will be discussed in relation to the U.K. case in order to develop an understanding of the Benchmark Case.

United Kingdom

The first most significant event within the early phase of the U.K. case was the establishment of the Efficiency Unit. This view, which has been put forward by Metcalfe (1993), can be interpreted using the explanatory framework outlined previously in this chapter. Baumgartner and Jones would describe this event as a change in the "policy subsystem," for it changed patterns of participation in the policy-making process and gave a new unit some prerogatives. New participants included the Efficiency Adviser, Derek Rayner, as well as prime minister Margaret Thatcher; her inclusion, in particular, constituted a dramatic change in the policy subsystem. In addition, the Efficiency Unit acquired the institutional prerogative to act directly within the area of methods as well as to propose changes in other areas of public management.[17]

What, then, explains the establishment of the Efficiency Unit? In addressing this question with reference to Kingdon's model, three related constructs are employed: policy entrepreneurship, the career of policy issues, and the three streams. The salient policy entrepreneur at this stage was plainly Margaret Thatcher, who can be credited with performing three functions of policy entrepreneurship: moving public management issues onto the governmental policy agenda, sharpening the problem definition, and creating a process for developing policy alternatives. As opposition leader, Thatcher had been an outspoken critic of the civil service, reinforcing the issue's standing on the systemic agenda. As prime minister, Thatcher demonstrated her interest in identifying policy solutions.[18] This stance marked the issue's progression to the governmental policy agenda. Apart from influencing the career progression and agenda status of public management issues, Thatcher engaged the problem stream. She sharpened the issue's definition in arguing that government organizations were inefficiently managed. However, there were few policy alternatives about. Among her intentions in establishing the Efficiency Unit was to add vitality to the policy stream. In sum, the explanation for this event lies in Thatcher's performance of several functions of policy entrepreneurship.[19]

The second most significant event within the early phase of the U.K. case was the launch of the Financial Management Initiative (FMI). Unlike the establishment of the Efficiency Unit, the FMI launch did not represent a material change in the policy subsystem. Rather, it was a discrete policy decision of the sort Kingdon's model is designed to explain. The broad explanation is that the political and problem streams remained stable, while more ideas came to circulate in the policy stream. The problem stream's stability is attributable to the policy subsystem centered on the Efficiency Unit. The Rayner scrutinies provided fresh evidence to support the argument that inefficiency was not just a condition but also a problem to be solved. In Levitt and March's terms, the scrutinies had the effect of reinforcing the motivation to search for measures to make government more efficient. The novel factor in this situation was discussions about how to apply mainstream thinking on managing decentralized organizations to central government, involving such concepts as centralization of goal setting, measurement of performance, expanded managerial discretion in budget execution, and responsibility centers. Policy entrepreneurship and organizational learning are part of the explanation. In this case, the policy entrepreneurs included Derek Rayner and Michael Heseltine. Both actively drew on private sector experience as well as that of the governmental organizations they headed: the Efficiency Unit, in Rayner's case, and the Department of the Environment, in Heseltine's. This organizational learning process is attributable to a combination of factors, including the definition of the problem as inefficient management in government, the related belief that the private sector operated more efficiently because of better management practices, and opportunities afforded by both men's senior position in government.

From a Kingdon perspective, the emergence of the FMI is at least partly explained by the process of transforming policy ideas into specific alternatives. This process included not only the Efficiency Unit, but also the Treasury. The involvement of the Treasury is attributable to the fact that its prerogatives were specifically related to ideas floating in the policy stream at the time. The political and problem streams, meanwhile, indicated the direction of policy-making. The Treasury's desire to protect its prerogatives may have contributed to its decision to join with the Efficiency Unit in crafting a concrete policy alternative as a follow-on to the Rayner scrutinies (Gray and Jenkins 1991; Zifcak 1994). Treasury support for this proposal in turn helped open the window of opportunity for a prime ministerial decision to launch the FMI, which prescribed changes in institutional rules and routines in the broadly defined area of financial management.

As we have seen, the explanation for the FMI includes the combined presence of several factors linked to the Efficiency Unit. These factors included a stable problem definition (specifically, the inefficient management of government departments), an organizational learning process centered on a strategically positioned staff organization (specifically, the conduct of the Rayner scrutinies and other activities of the Efficiency Unit), and "co-opetition" between staff organizations within the policy subsystem (specifically, the Efficiency Unit and the Treasury).[20] By this argument, a major effect of the Efficiency Unit's establishment was to increase the potential for policy change down the line. The specific link between this event and the FMI was its modification of the policy subsystem, a change that provided wider opportunities for actors sharing the prime minister's beliefs to perform the functions of policy entrepreneurship. Among the key entrepreneurial functions performed by actors located in this modified policy subsystem were reinforcing the problem definition, cultivating "new" policy ideas, and crafting specific policy proposals.

Australia

The most significant single public management policy event during the 1982–1986 period was the formal launch of the Financial Management Improvement Program (FMIP). The FMIP and the United Kingdom's Financial Management Initiative were substantively similar: both involved changes in institutional rules and routines in the area of financial management.[21]

Explanations for these policy choices are, in general terms, also similar: Public management issues were included on the governmental policy agenda; the policy problem was defined in terms of organizational inefficiency in government; and the policy stream was stocked with managerial ideas about how to change the administrative systems of government, especially in financial management. These three factors are therefore candidates for inclusion in an explanatory account of the Benchmark Case.

A more detailed explanation reveals further commonalities as well as some differences. The inclusion of public management issues on the governmental policy agenda in both cases is attributable to parallel changes in the political stream—specifically, the election of the Conservatives in Britain in 1979 and that of the Labor Party in Australia in 1982. Before coming to power, Thatcher was a vociferous critic of the civil service, while Australia's Labor Party experimented with public management changes at the state level. Their assumption of office provided an opportunity to perform the entrepreneurial function of placing public management issues on the central government policy agenda.

However, similar problem definitions in Australia and the United Kingdom were reached via different routes. In the United Kingdom, a major factor determining the emergence of the face of the policy issue was Thatcher's conviction that the civil service was rife with inefficiency and led by poor managers. In Australia, a comparable explanatory role is played by policy spillover effects (Walker 1977; Kingdon 1984). The center-left Labor government was concerned by foreseeable consequences of fiscal austerity on clients of public services. The government's desire to mitigate the impact of budget cutbacks entered the problem stream as a belief that efficiency must be substantially improved.[22] The primary link between the change in government and the problem definition was thus less direct in Australia than in the United Kingdom: in Australia, the problem's definition was primarily a spillover from macroeconomic/fiscal policy, whereas in the United Kingdom, Thatcher's conviction that the civil service was a poorly managed and inefficient set of organizations served as the primary link.[23] However, in both cases, the policy streams were influenced by broadly similar processes, including vicarious and direct learning. Managerial ideas were pumped into the policy stream by the Reid committee, Finance department officials, and central agency ministers in Australia and notably by the Efficiency Unit in the United Kingdom. Policy-makers also looked to governmental experience. While the learning processes were broadly similar in the two cases, the U.K. case differed in that this process was stimulated by a decisive change in the policy subsystem: the Efficiency Unit was a new staff unit, whereas the Reid Commission was a temporary advisory body. The Labor government did not change the policy subsystem as part of its effort to influence the direction of public management policy, although it should be mentioned that the Finance department was split from the Treasury in 1976. This difference can be attributed to the United Kingdom's and Australia's respective points of departure as well as some contemporaneous factors.[24]

In sum, this explanation of two parallel policy events—the FMI and the FMIP—indicates broadly similar agenda-setting and alternative-specification dynamics in the United Kingdom and Australia. The similarities are apparent in access of public management issues to the governmental policy agenda, problem definition, and the policy stream. A subtle difference in the two cases is that the FMIP was more like a policy spillover in Australia than was the FMI in the United Kingdom.

New Zealand

The most significant single event during the early phase of the New Zealand case of public management policy-making was a Treasury briefing to government following Labour's reelection in 1987, entitled "Government Management." This briefing called for radical reform of public management policies in New Zealand, focusing on the institutional rules governing financial management, civil service and labor relations, and organization. The proposals led to enactment of two major bills during Labour's second term in office and to the rapid implementation of the changes in formulated management policies (Boston et al. 1991; Schick 1996; Kettl 1997).

The explanation for this event is similar to that of the U.K. and Australia cases in its broad outlines: Public sector management issues arrived on the governmental policy agenda as a result of a change in government (the Labour party's victory in 1983); the problem came to be defined in terms of organizational inefficiency; and the policy stream was stocked with ideas about how to solve this problem. At the next level of detail, the New Zealand case shares properties with the early phases of the U.K. and Australia cases. The most clear-cut similarities between the New Zealand and the U.K. cases are, first, the direct route from beliefs to problem definition and, second, the conspicuous performance of the functions of policy entrepreneurship. The most evident similarities between the New Zealand and Australia cases are, first, spillovers from economic to public management policy and, second, stability in the policy subsystem.

The source of the problem's definition in New Zealand was the Treasury's professional staff. Like Thatcher, New Zealand's Treasury officials were convinced that government departments, as well as other parts of the state sector, were inefficient. However, the basis for their respective convictions is a matter of some dispute among observers. Some argue that both Thatcher and officials in the New Zealand Treasury were influenced by public choice ideas, including the argument that bureaucrats strive to maximize budgets. Other observers lay stress on Thatcher's visceral aversion to the civil service culture and on her sanguine views of private sector management. The view of New Zealand Treasury officials, by contrast, was rooted in their professional training as economists. Their conviction that government departments were inefficient may have rested more on agency theory than on other strands of the New Institutional Economics, such as Niskanen's budget-maximizing bureaucrat thesis, which came to Thatcher's attention.[25] These case differences can be regarded as historical details for the purposes of the discussion thus far: the main effect of the convictions held by the New Zealand Treasury and Thatcher was to define the policy problem as one of inefficient government organizations.[26]

The argument that economic policy spilled over into public management policy in both Australia and New Zealand is worth elaborating on. These spillover effects were different in their details. In Australia, the intersection of center-left ideology and fiscal austerity generated the problem of governmental inefficiency: this spillover linked economic policies to the *problem* stream. In New Zealand, by contrast, the main spillover was from economic policy to the *policy* stream. This spillover is symbolized by the Treasury's packaging of "Government Management" as a sequel to its briefing to the incoming Labour government in 1984 entitled "Economic Management." Explaining this spillover effect brings to light distinctive properties of the policymaking process in New Zealand: the policy subsystem fit Baumgartner and Jones's definition of a policy monopoly (unlike in the United Kingdom after the establishment of the Efficiency Unit); the Treasury was responsible for economic policy as well as budgeting and financial management (unlike the case of the Finance Department in Australia); and the Treasury was staffed by recently trained professional economists (unlike the U.K. Treasury).[27] The situation in New Zealand provided an ideal context for economic policy to spill over into public management.

Like the FMI and FMIP, the explanation for proposals put to government in New Zealand can be expressed in terms of policy entrepreneurship. In all three cases, actors at the center of government performed the entrepreneurial functions of advancing the career of public management issues, defining policy problems, generating policy alternatives, and placing proposals on central decision makers' decisional agenda. The New Zealand case stands out as one where the functions of entrepreneurship were substantially performed by one organization: the Treasury. In other cases, these entrepreneurial functions were performed by more actors working from a slightly wider array of institutional platforms. An institutional explanation for this display of policy entrepreneurship is the "post-colonial" structure and style of New Zealand's central government in the early 1980s (Campbell 1997). Focusing on these details, however, is a diversion for the present research task (see figure 2). The broad point is that central decision makers and central staff units were able to arrange for the problem, policy, and political streams to converge—and their actions contributed to similarities in the problem and policy streams. At this level of abstraction, the narratives are broadly similar, even as the cases differ in their details.

THE BENCHMARK CASES: LATER REFORM PHASES

This section examines subsequent phases of the benchmark cases with the aim of completing the explanation of their similar outcome.

United Kingdom

The single most important policy event in the U.K. case was the launching of the Next Steps initiative in 1987. Government departments were given the opportunity to structure their operational components as executive agencies, headed by chief executives serving on fixed-term contracts and reporting directly to ministers. The candidate pool for these jobs was to include private sector managers, executives in the public sector, and civil servants. Financial management rules were to be tailored to the circumstances of each executive agency through framework agreements set up with the Treasury. Taken as a whole, Next Steps was broader in scope than were previous initiatives, changing government-wide institutional routines in civil service, organization, and financial management.

Next Steps is attributable to stability in the political and problem streams and dynamism in the policy stream, a similar combination of factors as the FMI: in 1987, Thatcher was prime minister and organizational inefficiency was still deemed a policy problem; the dynamism of the policy stream was due to organizational learning by participants in the public management policy subsystem.[28] Direct learning focused on implementation of FMI. In time, the benefits of this initiative were judged to be meager. Some of the dissatisfaction centered on uneven levels of ministerial involvement in the public management process. The doctrine that ministers are managers, which had always been viewed with some skepticism, became discredited.[29] Other concerns centered on the seeming unwillingness of departmental officials to decentralize responsibility for budget execution. This mismatch between reality and aspirations led to a renewed search for policy alternatives.[30]

Through vicarious learning, attention was drawn to the divisionalized form of organizational structure that is prevalent among multiproduct firms (Mintzberg 1983). In this type of structure, major operating units are designated as divisions, their general managers are considered fully responsible and accountable for unit-level performance, and top executives in the corporate office primarily exercise a form of output control over the divisions. The process of vicarious organizational learning led to the belief that divisionalization of government departments would be a more effective solution to the efficiency problem than continuing the FMI would be. Following the divisional model, ministers' role would be like that of top executives in the corporate office, and the role of agency chief executives would be like that of division general managers. The fundamental policy idea of divisionalizing government departments was elaborated through the alternative-specification process. The FMI's attempt to change organizational culture without altering recruitment and selection of personnel, for instance, was abandoned in favor of opening up chief executive positions to non–civil servants. The employment regime for chief executives was distinguished from that of the civil service. The resulting proposal, built on the chassis of the divisional model, arrived on the decisional agenda in 1987 and received the prime minister's approval.

During the 1990s, under the Conservative government of John Major, a number of other significant policy events occurred in the United Kingdom, including the launch of the Citizens Charter initiative and the Competing for Quality effort. These events are significant theoretically because they contributed to the case outcome of comprehensive public management policy change. The Citizens Charter initiative changed institutional rules in the areas of audit and evaluation, while Competing for Quality changed institutional rules in procurement and methods. The cumulative effect of these initiatives and those of the 1980s was to change institutional rules in five areas: expenditure planning and financial management, civil service and labor relations, procurement, organization and methods, and audit and evaluation.

The Citizens Charter initiative was attributable to dynamics in all three streams of the policy-making process. Instability in the political stream was due to the desire of the Conservative party leader, John Major, to define himself as different from Margaret Thatcher. Raising the issue of citizen satisfaction with public services during the 1992 election was a means to this end. Major's discourse, in effect, transformed concerns about service quality into a policy problem. The alternative-specification process from which the Citizens Charter initiative emerged was informed by ideas and practices of business process management and, in this sense, involved vicarious learning. In broad outline, then, the explanation for the Citizens Charter is similar to that of the Efficiency Unit. Change occurred in the political stream, which flowed directly into the problem stream; furthermore, the prime minister was personally involved in arranging for all three of Kingdon's streams to intersect.

The ramifications of the Citizens Charter for public management policy-making echo those of the Efficiency Unit as well. Major established a unit within the Cabinet Office dedicated to managing the Citizens Charter initiative. In Baumgartner and Jones's terms, this decision equates to a change in the policy subsystem dealing with public management policy. This policy subsystem also evolved as a result of establishing a ministerial post within the Cabinet Office, with direct oversight of the Next Steps implementation team, the Citizens Charter Unit, and the Efficiency Unit. The effect of this evolution, according to Campbell and Wilson (1995), was to provide William Waldegrave—the minister appointed to this post—with an opportunity to devote full attention to the governmental policy agenda in public management and to perform several of the interlocking functions of policy entrepreneurship.

By the mid-1990s, the U.K. case had settled into a partial equilibrium. Public management issues, while they remained on the governmental policy agenda, were largely processed within the policy subsystem. Describing this situation as a partial equilibrium does not imply a slackening in policy-making activity in public management. Indeed, the partial equilibrium of the 1990s

Box 2. Factors in the Partial Equilibrium Situation

A. Kingdon's model

A1. Political Stream	Broadly stable
A2. Problem Stream	Broadly stable
A3. Policy Stream	Dynamic
A4. Policy Choices	Ongoing flow

B. Baumgartner and Jones's model

B1. Policy Subsystem	Unsegmented
B2. Domain Structure	Unified
B3. Issue Image	Organizational inefficiency across government

C. Levitt and March's model

C1. Aspiration Levels	High and stable
C2. Satisfaction Levels	Low and stable
C3. Search Process	Active
C4. Actions	Ongoing flow
C5. Outcomes	Ongoing flow

provided for a continuing flow of policy actions, such as the launch of the Competing for Quality effort, the Private Finance Initiative, and the Resource Accounting and Budgeting project. In this sense, the situation of partial equilibrium is closely linked to the case outcome of comprehensive public management policy change.[31]

Providing an analytic description of the partial equilibrium situation will shed light on the reasons for the case outcome. This description draws on the three models built into the explanatory framework. Box 2 identifies the conceptual elements of each model and indicates their respective status in a situation of partial equilibrium. The question is what explains the Policy Choices (A4). The answer is stated in terms of a model of the partial equilibrium scenario.

The abstract account provided in Box 3 coheres with research on the United Kingdom, although much more analysis of this particular case can be provided. The immediate question, however, is whether this stylized account of the policy-making process applies to the other two cases that comprise the Benchmark Case. The next section examines the Australia and New Zealand cases with this analytic question in mind.

Australia

In the period from 1987 through the mid-1990s, Australia experienced comprehensive public management policy change. A major reorganization of the machinery of government was declared. As discussed in chapter 2, this decision consolidated departments, established a two-tier ministry, and expanded the range of public management policy instruments under the control of government ministers by abolishing the Public Service Board. In the area of expenditure planning and financial management, institutional rules and routines evolved through the Financial Management Improvement Program (FMIP) and its sister effort, Program Management and Budgeting. Changes in the civil service and labor relations area were put into place primarily

Box 3. The Partial Equilibrium Scenario

1. Organizational inefficiency and related problems are constantly found in the Problem Stream (A2).
    The content and stability of the Problem Stream (A2) are due to the Policy Subsystem (B1) and the Political Stream (A1).
        The exercise of the Policy Subsystem's (B1) prerogatives reinforces the belief that inefficiency is a policy problem.
        The Policy Subsystem's (B1) stability depends on that of the Political Stream (A1).

2. The Policy Stream (A3) is dynamic.
    The Policy Stream is dynamic because the Search (C3) for policy alternatives is continually active, for several reasons.
    A. Satisfaction (C2) with the rules and routines comprising public management policy is not attained.
       Dissatisfaction is due to high and stable Aspiration Levels (C1) and to the ambiguity of the Outcomes (C5) of Policy Choice (A4, C4).
    B. The Policy Subsystem (B1) possesses the organizational capacity to engage in continual search effort.
    C. The Policy Subsystem (B1) is expected to draw inferences from the Outcomes (C5) of its Actions (C4) and from vicarious organizational experiences.
    D. The active Search Process (C3) provides a regular flow of policy ideas, ranging across all subdomains of public management policy.

Box 3. The Partial Equilibrium Scenario *(continued)*

E. These policy ideas are automatically channeled into the Policy Stream (A3), since the Policy Subsystem (B1) performs both search and alternative specification.

3. Policy decisions are made.
The Policy Subsystem (B1) uses its prerogatives both to make Policy Choices (A4) and to place alternatives on the decisional agenda of central decision makers who make the policy decisions.

through the government's "structural adjustment" policy and its implementation of enterprise-level bargaining within the public service. Significant changes in procurement occurred through major reform of the Department of Administrative Services. Routines in the area of audit and evaluation were changed as a result of innovation within the Australian National Audit Office as well as the implementation of Program Management and Budgeting. Taken as a whole, these changes modified institutional rules in all areas of public management policy.

The partial equilibrium model describes the Australia case after the 1987 machinery of government reorganization. The Policy Subsystem (B1) was stable once the reorganization was put into effect. This subsystem included several departments: Finance, Prime Minister and Cabinet, Administrative Services, and Industrial Relations as well as the Australian National Audit Office. Meanwhile, the Policy Stream (A3) was dynamic as a result of the

Search Process (C3), which was active for the same reasons described in the partial equilibrium model (e.g., direct and vicarious learning within the Policy Subsystem). The results of the search process fed into the policy stream; ideas became policy alternatives; and policy alternatives became decisions.

This interpretation is especially plausible for changes in the areas of expenditure planning and financial management, procurement, and audit and evaluation. However, the same is less true for changes in civil service and labor relations. Changes in the rules and routines of position classification, for instance, were brought about through the public sector's counterpart of the economic "structural adjustment" policy (Campbell and Halligan 1992). The latter aimed to make the economy efficient through deregulation, removal of subsidies, privatization, and sectoral plans for increasing productivity. The subsequent decision to pursue a policy of structural adjustment within government has all the markings of a policy spillover. The same can be said for enterprise bargaining. This policy made the enterprise—as opposed to the nation as a whole—the level at which wage bargains were struck in the commercial sector. In time, the government adopted enterprise bargaining for the public service so that labor agreements were negotiated by departments or their major components. In these two instances—structural adjustment and enterprise bargaining —the dynamism of the policy stream is more attributable to spillovers from economic to public management policy than to the learning process described by the partial equilibrium model.

The model of the partial equilibrium situation thus coheres with some, but not all, key pieces of evidence about the Australia case. The changes in the civil service and labor relations area, as well as in organization, are better explained using other constructs. For this purpose, the accounts of Pusey (1991) and Campbell and Halligan (1992), surveyed in the previous chapter, are needed. Key ideas discussed in those works are economic rationalism and executive leadership: both factors were present and reinforcing in the Australia case. Economic rationalism, viewed as a policy paradigm (Hall 1992), made it natural for economic policies—such as structural adjustment and enterprise bargaining —to be translated into policy ideas for public management. The executive leadership factor describes the high degree of interaction and cooperation among ministers and officials at the center of government. The intersection of the economic rationalism and executive leadership factors explains the policy spillovers between economic policy and the civil service and labor relations area of public management policy. This scenario should be kept in mind in fashioning an explanation of the Benchmark Case outcome.

New Zealand

New Zealand is known for its big bang approach to changing public management policy. Comprehensive public management policy change occurred as the result of what could be considered a discrete policy event, namely the formulation of proposals put forth in the Treasury's 1987 postelection briefing on "Government Management" and the subsequent policy decisions based on it. This event produced changes in expenditure planning and financial management (e.g., output budgeting and accrual accounting), civil service and labor relations (e.g., configuring the rules and routines surrounding the appointment, removal, and compensation of departmental chief executives), organization (e.g., machinery of government changes based on the principle of separating policy advice and service provision), procurement (e.g., facilitating decisions to contract out), and auditing and evaluation (e.g., performance agreements between ministers, the State Services Commission, and chief executives). This scenario is perhaps best explained using Kingdon's model, which, as discussed earlier in this chapter, focuses on discrete policy events.

The partial equilibrium model is fairly descriptive of the New Zealand case in the 1990s. During this time, the Policy Subsystem (B1) actively searched for ways to refine routines in the area of expenditure planning and financial management as well as in civil service and labor relations (Schick 1996). For instance, the State Services Commission (SSC) initiated a government-wide process to provide a strategic context for expenditure planning, while the Treasury and SSC developed new procedures for holding chief executives accountable for executing their performance plans. The active search for new routines was based on stability in the Policy Subsystem (B1), a unified public management policy domain (B2), and a stable issue image (B3).

A Common Narrative?

The previous dialogue between explanatory ideas and case evidence suggests that both the disequilibrium and partial equilibrium scenarios are apparent in all three instances of comprehensive public management policy change. The disequilibrium scenario describes the initial agenda-setting dynamics through which public management issues gained access to governmental policy agendas and organizational efficiency became fixed as the face of the issue. As we have seen, the problem stream was highly sensitive to changes in the political stream, and relatedly, central decision makers performed functions of policy entrepreneurship. In the U.K. and New Zealand cases, in particular, central decision makers' conviction that the core public sector was inefficient provided an impetus for performing these entrepreneurial functions.[32] The specific policy alternatives generated by the policy stream during the disequilibrium scenario were not identical across cases, except in the abstract sense of altering the institutional rules and routines that comprise public management policy. The "institutional" outcome of the disequilibrium scenario was very similar, however: the policy subsystem became focused within central agencies, the issue image was closely related to organizational inefficiency, and the domain structure reflected the belief that public management policies were highly interrelated.[33]

The partial equilibrium scenario describes the U.K. case after the launch of the Citizens Charter in 1992, aspects of the Australia case after 1987, and the New Zealand case in the 1990s. In this scenario, the policy subsystem/issue image/domain structure configuration was stable, while the policy stream was dynamic. This dynamism was due to an active search for options to change institutional rules or routines within and across the public management policy domain. The active search was due to high aspirations supported by the political stream, the organizational capacity of the policy subsystem, and the belief that public management policies needed to be managed as a system. The search involved direct learning and, to varying degrees, vicarious learning as well. The fact that the same policy subsystem conducted the search process, transformed policy ideas into policy alternatives, and enjoyed substantial prerogatives as policy-making moved into the decisional stage helps to explain why active search led to a flow of policy choices.

The previous two paragraphs offer a serviceable account of the Benchmark Case. The narrative of this composite case includes both the disequilibrium and partial equilibrium scenarios, each linked to a configuration of factors identified in the explanatory framework. In the most stylized version of the Benchmark Case, the disequilibrium scenario is followed by the partial equilibrium one, and the sequence explains comprehensive public management policy change.

By design, this account of the Benchmark Case suppresses differences among the underlying cases. The U.K. case is plausibly interpreted as two consecutive cycles, with the first sequence of disequilibrium/partial equilibrium describing 1980 to 1991 and the second describing 1992 to the victory of New Labour in 1997. In contrast, the New Zealand case appears to display a single cycle. These and other differences among the underlying cases are worth bearing in mind as the Benchmark Case is used for purposes of comparative analysis, to which we now turn.

BROADENING GENERALIZATIONS THROUGH COMPARISON

In this section, brief discussions of three further cases—Sweden, the United States, and Germany—are provided. The central aim is to indicate how an understanding of public policy-making in the public management domain can be enlarged through comparative research methods. That understanding consists of insight about the individual cases as well as generalizations drawn from an explanation of similarities and differences among them.

Sweden

In Sweden, substantial change in public management policy occurred in the 1980s and 1990s. Institutional rules and routines were altered in the areas of expenditure planning and financial management (e.g., development of a running cost system), civil service and labor relations (e.g., decentralization of collective bargaining to executive agencies), and audit and evaluation (e.g., expansion of performance auditing). Sweden appears to be another instance of comprehensive public management policy change.[34] What explains the broadly similar outcomes in Sweden and the Benchmark Case?

The early 1980s in Sweden resembles the Benchmark Case disequilibrium scenario. The founding of the Civildepartment, mentioned in chapter 2, amounted to a change in the Policy Subsystem (B1), and a new Issue Image (B3) came into focus: central government's excessive regulation of local public service provision. As in the Benchmark Case, Sweden's interlocked changes in B1 and B3 were brought about by the Political Stream (A1), specifically, the attempt by the Social Democratic Party to shore up electoral support. The main policy event resulting from this disequilibrium situation was the Free Commune Experiment.

Decisions amounting to comprehensive public management policy change occurred during the late 1980s and early 1990s. At the time, the Swedish Social Democratic Party was seeking to reestablish its status as the natural party of government in the face of waning support from industrial workers. In the traded goods sector, which included industry, profits and wages were being squeezed by both international competition and the increased costs of non–traded goods. In the non–traded goods sector, wages were increasing faster than productivity. The public sector was implicated in this problem, since a major component of non–traded goods in Sweden is publicly provided. The relative lack of discipline in the non–traded goods sector came to be seen not only as damaging to international competitiveness but also as unfair. In reaching out for support from capital and labor in the traded goods sector, the Social Democrats took on the problem of public sector inefficiency (Schwartz 1994a, 1994b; Barzelay and Hassel 1994).

This newly defined policy problem generated another disequilibrium situation. The impulse for change in public management policy was most immediately felt in the Ministry of Finance (MoF), which took on the task of generating policy alternatives that responded to the problem of inefficiency. Indeed, the MoF was the main platform for exercising policy entrepreneurship in public management. Proposals were generated in the areas of expenditure planning and financial management, civil service and labor relations, and audit and evaluation. The impression derived from the literature on this period in Sweden is that the situation later became that of a partial equilibrium, with a continual search for alternatives to refine routines, for example, in linking auditing to expenditure planning and financial management (OECD 1996).

Because Sweden is broadly similar to the Benchmark Case, comparisons with the latter's underlying cases are of some analytic interest. Sweden and the United Kingdom display parallels in their initial stages. Soon after assuming power, central decision makers modified the Policy Subsystem (B1): in Sweden, the Social Democrats established the Civildepartment, while Thatcher established the Efficiency Unit in the United Kingdom. These units operated as platforms for policy entrepreneurship. Their work resulted in clearer definitions of the policy problem and well-developed policy alternatives. Differences in downstream policy events—in other words, the Free Commune Experiment and the Financial Management Initiative—reflect the distinctive casts of the policy problems in Sweden and the United Kingdom as they were defined at the time.

Striking parallels between Sweden and Australia are apparent in the late 1980s. In both cases, public management policy change was closely linked to economy-wide reforms; the links appear to have been even more direct than in the United Kingdom and perhaps even New Zealand. In Australia, broad-banding the position classification system and decentralizing collective bargaining were spillovers from the economic "structural adjustment" policy and the industrial relations policy of enterprise bargaining, respectively. In Sweden, giving agencies responsibility for collective bargaining with trade unions was a direct spillover from that country's reversal in economic and labor policies. In both cases, the spillover effect was energized by the Political Stream (A1).

United States

The U.S. federal government during the 1980s and 1990s displays many similarities with the Benchmark Case, as change was strongly evident in most areas of public management policy. Institutional rules and organizational routines in the area of audit and evaluation were affected by the Government Results and Performance Act, the Chief Financial Officers Act, and the National Performance Review's service quality initiative. Change was also evident in the area of procurement, with legislative changes known as "procurement streamlining" and major changes in routines within the General Services Administration. To some degree, change was evident in the area of civil service and labor relations, with rules and routines developed to downsize the federal workforce and to reform the Office of Personnel Management. The reinvention labs initiative constituted a change in the area of organization and methods. However, no major reorganization of the federal bureaucracy has occurred.

The policy-making process in the United States bears some resemblance to the disequilibrium scenario describing the Benchmark Case. The Political Stream (A1)—specifically the 1992 election and the subsequent launch of Clinton's presidency—generated the policy problem of making government "work better and cost less." Against the background of the Reagan and Bush presidencies, the "works better" concept represented a change in the problem definition, from one of the size of government to its efficiency. The change in problem definition was interlocked with alterations in Domain Structure (B2) and the Policy Subsystem (B1). The domain of public management policy was largely unified by the National Performance Review (NPR): the NPR's argumentation reflected the view that public management policies were highly interrelated, thereby counseling that they be managed in a systematic manner. The NPR itself represented a change in the Policy Subsystem, being separate from other central agencies such as the Office of Management and Budget (OMB). The continual involvement of Vice President Al Gore in public management policy-making also indicated that some change in the Policy Subsystem (B1) had occurred.

These interlocking elements of a disequilibrium scenario account for the highly active Search (C3) for alternatives that followed the launch of the NPR in 1993. The Search Process put the Government Performance and Results Act, which had been sponsored by a Republican senator, on the presidential decision agenda. The Search Process also led to specification of policy alternatives in the area of procurement: the institutional platform for performing this entrepreneurial function was the Office of Federal Procurement Policy, a unit of OMB.[35] In both instances, the eventual effect was to change public management policy.

Still, the partial equilibrium scenario seems to characterize the Clinton presidency after the 1994 midterm Congressional election. In partial equilibrium, the Search Process (C3) remained active because of a configuration of stable Aspirations (C1), the organizational capacity of the Policy Subsystem (B1), and the Political Stream (A1) (i.e., presidential electoral politics), and a flow of Actions (C4) followed.[36]

From a research perspective, the United States is an awkward case. The utility of this case is likely to arise from two kinds of comparisons. One type involves comparison with the benchmark cases using a less abstract definition of the case outcome than comprehensive public management policy change. Research along these lines might attempt to account for the United States's relative lack of change in areas of financial management and organization; the similar levels of change in the area of audit and evaluation; and the apparently more substantial degree of change in the area of procurement. A second type of comparison involves reference to non–benchmark cases. Considered as a case of near-comprehensive change, the United States might be compared with cases where change has been much less comprehensive, such as in the German federal government. Either way, the U.S. case, when analyzed comparatively, will be useful for developing limited historical generalizations.

Germany

By all accounts, Germany in the 1980s and 1990s is not a case of comprehensive public management policy change. This difference compared with the Benchmark Case makes developments in the German federal government analytically interesting. The main explanation for this difference is that a disequilibrium scenario apparent in the Benchmark Case did not occur in the German case. A factor that might have initiated such a disequilibrium scenario in Germany was the change in government in 1982, when the CDU-CSU-FDP coalition under Chancellor Helmut Kohl replaced the SPD-FDP coalition under Helmut Schmidt. Therefore, the question is why was the public management policy-making process in Germany left undisturbed by this change in the Political Stream (A1)?[37]

Once the Benchmark Case has been used to frame the analytic issue, comparisons can be made between its underlying cases and that of Germany. If the United Kingdom is the specific point of comparison, an explanation might lie in the fact that Thatcher played the role of policy entrepreneur in the area of public management, whereas Kohl did not. The question then is what accounts for this difference: following Elster (1998), the actors' opportunities and beliefs should be considered. The opportunities available to the German chancellor to exercise influence over the Policy Subsystem (B1) are more constrained than in the

United Kingdom because of coalition politics, but the opportunities to influence the Problem Stream (A2) are comparable. Since opportunities are similar in some respects, the actors' beliefs should be examined. Kohl did not believe that the German civil service should be shaken up, whereas Thatcher was convinced that the British civil service was in dire need of change. What, in turn, explains this difference in belief? The argument that Thatcher was highly influenced by public choice ideas is relevant in this connection, as is her view that the private sector was more efficient than the civil service. Kohl's softer views might be attributed, in part, to the fact that civil servants comprise a large fraction of the Bundestag, the lower house of Parliament.

The German case can usefully be compared with the New Zealand one as well. The main analytic question again is why a disequilibrium situation emerged in New Zealand but not in Germany. The sources of disequilibrium in New Zealand included the conjuncture of a change in government and an economic crisis followed by a massive reversal in economic policies, which spilled over into the public management domain. When Kohl became chancellor in 1982, the German economy was suffering a sharp economic recession, but not of the order of the economic crisis in New Zealand, and the economy began to improve as early as 1983. Although the Kohl government sought to cut back on public expenditures, it did not seek to perform a major overhaul on economic policies at the same time. For these reasons, economic policy change did not spill over into public management policy.

German unification in 1990 was a sufficiently strong impulse to set in motion a disequilibrium process. However, the effects on public management policy at the federal level were muted.[38]

The German government did establish a temporary body in 1995 to generate policy alternatives, called the Lean State Expert Council. However, the council did not markedly change the Policy Subsystem (B1), which remained segmented: the Finance ministry was responsible for money-related issues, while the Interior ministry was responsible for personnel-related issues. The principle of departmental autonomy appears to have been honored, even by the chancellery, which enjoys the prerogative to coordinate the ministries.[39]

Why did the chancellery choose not to exercise its prerogatives? An institutional-type explanation is coalition politics. The finance minister belonged to the CSU while the interior minister was a CDU leader. Achieving coordination on this matter could have been costly. A processual-type explanation is agenda congestion. Policy-makers' attention was absorbed by such high-profile issues as German unification, European integration, and reform in some substantive policy areas. Another processual explanation is policy interference effects—the mirror image of policy spillovers. The prospect of public management policy change was unappealing during unification, as it might raise questions about the policy of transferring West Germany's administrative arrangements to Länder in the former German Democratic Republic.

The German case is thus one where the partial equilibrium situation in public management policy-making was left undisturbed by the 1982 election and unification, which were major events in the political stream (A1). In theory, comprehensive public management policy change could have occurred under a partial equilibrium: the association between disequilibrium and the Benchmark Case outcome is only a historical generalization.

The comparative analysis suggests why it did not occur. In the Benchmark Case, the partial equilibrium situation that obtained during the 1990s was supported by a unified public management policy domain (B2), an issue image of inefficiency (B3), and a policy subsystem (B1) in which all the organizations responsible for public management policy-making fall under the control of the cabinet and in which the government is formed by a single political party. In Germany, the policy subsystem (B1) is different from the policy subsystem in the Benchmark Case: it might be described as segmented because the Finance and Interior ministries are organizationally autonomous from one another and their ministers are typically drawn from different elements of the coalition government. In addition, there is little evidence that the public management policy domain (B2) is unified. As public management policies in Germany are not considered to be highly interrelated, policy-makers presumably do not aspire to manage them as a system. Why? One plausible explanation is the legalistic ethos of the German federal bureaucracy; another is the belief that administrative rules and routines should be modified in conjunction with the redesign of governmental programs (Katzenstein 1987; Derlien 1996); a third is well-documented tendencies toward decentralization within the German federal bureaucracy.

This account of the German case is not intended to be definitive, but rather is intended to illustrate the analytic benefits of using theories of the policy-making process as well as comparative methods to study the New Public Management.[40] This case adds confidence, first, to the generalization, based on the Benchmark Case, that the sequence of disequilibrium and partial equilibrium explains comprehensive public management policy change and, second, to the generalization that a situation of partial equilibrium is conducive to this outcome when at least two factors—an unsegmented policy subsystem (B1) and a unified public management policy domain (B2)—intersect. Applying the same approach to other cases whose outcomes differ markedly from that of the Benchmark Case is surely one way to expand empirical knowledge about public management policymaking.

CHAPTER SUMMARY

This chapter provides a research design for the comparative analysis of public management policy change. Against the baseline of single case studies, including those surveyed in chapter 2, the added value of the research approach taken here lies in its potential to yield generalizations.[41] These findings are statements about the configuration of factors affecting whether comprehensive public management policy change occurs. The explanation is the result of a certain dialogue between theoretical ideas and case evidence—a novel one for the subject of public management policy but not for other fields of public policy.[42]

The theoretical ideas entering the dialogue are processual models of public policy-making (Kingdon 1984; Baumgartner and Jones 1993) and organizational learning (Levitt and March 1990) as well as methods of comparative case analysis (Ragin 1987). These models, which stem from the same theoretical roots, are integrated into a framework tailored to fit both the research objective and policy area. The case evidence examined from this standpoint is drawn from previous research by fellow scholars.

The dialogue between ideas and evidence was directed to answering three questions. First, why did the same outcome occur in the benchmark cases? Second, why was the outcome in the Sweden and U.S. cases broadly similar to that in the composite Benchmark Case? Finally, why did comprehensive public management policy change *not* occur in Germany—in other words, what explains the different outcomes in the Germany case and the Benchmark Case?

The dialogue developed here concludes that comparative public management policy change is explained by a sequence of two types of situations: a disequilibrium in the public management policy-making process, followed by a partial equilibrium situation. Key questions are what explains, first, the emergence of a disequilibrium situation and, second, the flow of policy choices in the subsequent partial equilibrium situation. Disequilibrium situations result from such interlocking factors as a sharp change in the defined policy problem and a modification of the policy subsystem. Contributing factors are impulses emanating from the political stream and policy entrepreneurs' beliefs and opportunities. Partial equilibrium situations are described by stability in the policy subsystem, stability of the policy domain structure, and stability in the issue image. The dynamism of the partial equilibrium situation is due to an active search process for policy alternatives. This activity is tied to high and stable aspirations, which contribute to policy-makers' dissatisfaction with the institutional rules and routines comprising public management policy. The belief—sometimes described as a conviction—that government organizations are inefficient, combined with the relative absence of meaningful indicators of overall improvement, also contribute to stable levels of dissatisfaction. The generation of policy alternatives across all areas of public management policy—expenditure planning and financial management, civil service and labor relations, procurement, organization and methods, and audit and evaluation—is explained by a configuration of a unified public management policy domain; an unsegmented policy subsystem; the issue image of inefficient government; and the inferences drawn from direct and vicarious experience. This complex of factors helps account for the opportunities open to those whose actions perform the function of policy entrepreneurship in the public management domain.

These modest historical generalizations (Ragin 1987) are relevant to policy-makers in evaluating whether a given course of action has the potential to bring about across-the-board changes in public management policy. A challenge for policy research on the New Public Management is therefore to improve upon the analysis and generalizations put forward in this chapter. Another such challenge is the focus of the rest of this book.

CHAPTER FOUR

How to Argue about the New Public Management

As an empirical matter, public management policy choices in the benchmark cases have been influenced by ideas entering the problem and policy streams from economics and management. For this reason, much scholarly commentary on NPM has revolved around how far public management policy choices *should be* influenced by such bodies of thought. Some critics of NPM have rejected the assumptions of economic models, while others have focused their concerns on the borrowing of management ideas and practices from the private sector (Pollitt 1993; Savoie 1994; Gregory 1995). Even writers sympathetic to NPM tend to evaluate whether ideas from economics and management are an adequate basis for making public management policy. Schick (1996), for example, argues that the strong points of New Zealand's reforms reflect management ideas, while the weak points grow out of the economic (contractualist) approach that predominated in that country's policy process in the 1980s.

In this chapter, attention shifts from the empirical analysis of change in public management policy to argumentation about ideas and policy choices in this domain. As we shall see, such argumentation about NPM has yet to mature into a policy-oriented dialogue; however, important steps in this direction have recently been taken. The aim of this chapter and the next is to provide a basis for dialogue about both doctrinal ideas and policy choices in the area of public management.

The point of departure is to discuss Peter Aucoin's (1995) *The New Public Management: Canada in Comparative Perspective*. Aucoin's book embodies a two-part thesis on how scholars should argue about NPM. The first part is that NPM discourse should span constitutional thought, empirical properties of executive government, principal-agent theory, beliefs about the effects of past administrative policies, and multicountry surveys of recent changes in public management policy; the second part of the thesis is that these considerations should, in turn, be brought to bear in evaluating public management policies.

Aucoin's study is an intellectually ambitious argument about public management policies. The study deserves close attention for two contrasting reasons: first, because it is a plausible model for such argumentation, and second, because its limitations make it a cautionary tale. The book could be a key point of reference for policy dialogue, provided that its argument is reconstructed along the lines indicated in this chapter. Had Aucoin's study exemplified good practices in argumentation such as those outlined in this chapter's final section, it might have generated a policy dialogue like that presented in chapter 5.

THE OVERALL PLAN OF AUCOIN'S ARGUMENT

Aucoin's book contrasts a favorable evaluation of public management policies implemented by New Zealand, the United Kingdom, and Australia during the 1980s and early 1990s with a critical evaluation of those adopted by Canada, and the author calls for Canada to catch up with the other three countries. To support these conclusions, Aucoin surveys practices in the four case study countries and develops a general argument about public management policy applicable to any Westminster system. This argument draws on ideas from the New Institutional Economics, management, and traditional public administration.

Writing as a public administrationist, Aucoin's overarching theme is "governance." His general position is that good governance requires that executive government be *(a)* politically responsible and *(b)* capable of formulating and implementing substantively valuable public policies. These two requirements, according to Aucoin, can only be satisfied if executive government includes a career civil service separate from and subordinate to the political executive (81).[1] However, he is quick to add that this institutional configuration, which is characteristic of Westminster-Whitehall systems, does not in itself guarantee responsible and good government; complementary, second-order conditions must also be satisfied to some degree for such an aspiration to be met.

To identify these second-order conditions, Aucoin turns to the question of how to manage the relationship between political executives and government departments staffed by the career public service. His broadest claim is that relations between political executives and the public service should be approached as if the intellectual task were to solve a principal-agent problem. He states that "relationships between ministers and their public servants are essentially relationships between principals and agents" (35).[2]

The third topic discussed by Aucoin is how to manage government departments. Here, the author incorporates the views expressed by Otto Brodtrick in a report on well-performing organizations issued by the Auditor General of Canada (169–170). Brodtrick identified four determinants of such organizations, labeled "emphasis on people," "participatory leadership," "innovative work styles," and "strong client orientation." Aucoin goes on to comment that, "The four emphases of well-performing organizations are hardly novel to normative management theory. Nevertheless, they are necessary ingredients of improved public management if public service organizations are to tap their most essential resource, namely the people who work in them" (170).

Aucoin's theoretical discussion is thus laid out in three tiers: addressing executive government corporately; relations between political executives and the public service; and management within government departments. The mapping between the tiers of Aucoin's discussion and the disciplinary source of each is roughly one-to-one. Public administration is the primary source of warrants for his claims about responsible and good government, which prescribes a career public service as a separate, subordinate, institution within executive government. Principal-agent theory is referred to as a key source of warrants about how to structure relations between political executives and the public service. And management is the primary source of ideas about the veritable detail of governance—internal management of government departments.

ANALYZING THE ARGUMENT

As discussed in the previous section, the claims about how political executives should engage the public service are apparently backed by warrants drawn from principal-agent theory.[3] Unfortunately, Aucoin's text does not discuss this strand of the New Institutional Economics in any detail, and the reader would have to consult works cited in the text. However, the footnotes make no reference to works by experts on principal-agent theory: James Q. Wilson, whom he does cite, does not qualify as such, while a cited work by Jonathan Boston (1991) is an analysis of the reasoning that influenced public management policy in New Zealand.[4] Without a firm grounding in principal-agent theory, readers would inevitably experience difficulty in discerning how (or even whether) Aucoin's claims about executive government are backed by warrants drawn from principal-agent theory.

What Aucoin might have written about principal-agent theory is as follows:

> Principal-agent theory is concerned with the economic analysis of relations between principals and agents. In the standard model, principals and agents do not share a common master, although many applications of principal-agent theory concern cases where principals and agents are locations within a formal organization. In the standard model, the principal-agent relationship is structured by means of a contract

that specifies how agents will be economically rewarded by their principals.[5] Within theoretical economics, principal-agent theory centers on the structuring of incentives, which are presumed to be the sole factor influencing agents' choice among alternative effort levels and actions.

A defining assumption of typical principal-agent models is that principals do not observe agents' actions or effort levels, either because of the physical impossibility of doing so or because of the excessive cost. The economic analysis of this type of situation quickly leads to an interim conclusion that rational principals provide agents with an incentive contract, normally described as a mathematical function relating an observed quantity to reward. The conventional term for the quantity chosen as a basis for reward is the agent's "output." Solving a principal-agent problem thus involves reaching an agreement that defines output.[6]

Analysis of principal-agent problems identifies considerations held by rational principals and agents during negotiations over the terms of "incentive" contracts, including the specification of output. One set of considerations is the quantities directly entering the utility functions of principals and agents. Another consideration is to avoid diluting the incentive effects of a reward scheme, as would be the case where outputs are specified ambiguously. A third consideration has to do with the allocation of and compensation for risk. Agents are at risk whenever the quantity defined as "output" varies as a function of factors other than their own actions or efforts. Rational agents demand compensation for bearing such risks. Principal-agent theory deals with how rational principals and agents will sort through such competing considerations to arrive at the terms of an incentive contract.

With this or similar background information, it is possible to critically discuss Aucoin's use of principal-agent theory. Aucoin puts forward three significant arguments about the role of political executives in public management that appear to be supported by principal-agent theory. First, since principals and agents rationally search for agreeable contractual terms to regulate their exchange relationships, responsible political executives and public servants correspondingly formulate "explicit contracts" to regulate their hierarchical relationship within executive government. Second, since rational principals specify outputs explicitly to render incentive effects, responsible political executives correspondingly define outputs explicitly to bring about a close alignment between public policy and the spending of public money. Third, since rational principals write contracts that provide automatic rewards on the basis of defined outputs, responsible political executives correspondingly hold the public service accountable for meeting output targets.[7]

Let's focus on the claim that responsible political executives provide explicit contracts specifying the output of the public service. Is the rationale for output-based contracts in government the same as that for output-based contracts in principal-agent theory? A standard rationale for output-based contracts in principal-agent theory is to compensate for the lack of observation of agents' actions. Aucoin's description of executive government, however, does not always match the assumption that principals do not observe agents' actions. Indeed, the problem he describes is one where too much effort has been devoted to monitoring the public service's actions, if not by ministers responsible for government departments, then by central staff or coordinating agencies. This mismatch between defining assumptions of agency theory and the description of government raises doubts about whether the former provides backing for Aucoin's claims about public management.

Aucoin's discussion of public management also makes little reference to incentives—an element central to agency theory. This fact raises the question whether the concept of "explicit contract" in Aucoin's hands is the same as the concept of "contract" in agency theory. The following passage suggests that contracts in public management are not incentives; they are agreements specifying shared aspirations for a department's accomplishments within a specified time frame:

> Improving public management . . . requires that managers, as agents, have explicit contracts or performance agreements with their ministers, or superiors, as their principals. . . . There must be an assertive cast of principals—that is, ministers—who, assisted by their policy advisers and corporate management support staff, set clear objectives, define concrete organizational missions, rigorous performance targets and measures and incorporate these in explicit principal-agent contracts or agreements. Agents are then given increased authority to deliver their outputs or programs and to manage their resources. (174)

Aucoin seems to have gravitated to a different concept of contract than is found in agency theory.

All told, the presentation does not make clear how agency theory is a basis for the conclusions Aucoin draws about public management. How, then, could Aucoin's argument be presented more clearly to a scholarly readership? More specifically, how might the argument be presented so that it is easily accessible to political scientists, economists, and management scholars? And how might the argument be presented so that it more closely relates to controversies surrounding NPM? To address these questions, it is useful to develop a model of Aucoin's argument.

SOME MODELING TERMINOLOGY

A preliminary step is to define what type of argument is under consideration. The discussion reviewed in the previous section could be called a "theory of public management policy." The term *theory*, however, has many meanings in the social sciences. To be clear about what we mean by theory, it is useful to set out how this concept relates to others in the literature on practical argumentation, public administration, and public policy, such as Toulmin (1958), Lindblom (1990), Hood and Jackson (1991), Walton (1992), and Dunn (1994).

> In the present context, *theory* refers generally to *arguments* about how to approach one or many *types of situations*. In the public management field, situations are routinely categorized in terms of *subject matter* and *institutional context*.
>
> Statements about a theory vary in terms of their role within any given unit of argument. These roles include *claims* and *warrants*. Warrants provide a basis for accepting that claims are plausible.

Within this frame of reference, the subject matter of Aucoin's theory is public management policy. The institutional context is Westminster-type governmental systems. The theory's claims are statements about considerations to be taken into account when evaluating or designing public management policy. The theory's warrants are the reasons to accept the theory's claims (e.g., statements drawn directly from agency theory).

As further clarification, allow me to underscore a distinction between "theory" and "policy arguments." Theory concerns types of situations, whereas evaluations and proposals pertain to particular situations. Accordingly, the claims of a theory are indefinite in their temporal horizon, whereas evaluations and proposals refer to the recent past, the present, and/or the immediate future. The latter is exemplified by Aucoin's favorable evaluation of NPM-style public management policies in the United Kingdom, New Zealand, and Australia, as well as by his proposals for improving public management policy in Canada's federal government.[8]

Observing this conceptual discussion, a linguist would say that "theory" and "policy argument" are being discussed as "paradigms." These paradigms can be represented schematically, as follows:

Theory	*Policy Argument*
Type of situation	Particular situation
Indefinite time frame	Specific periods
Analytical framework	Evaluations/proposals
Standing volitions	Action volitions
Argument	Argument
Warrants/presumptions	Warrants/presumptions
Claims/conclusions	Claims/conclusions

Using these terms, I will proceed to lay out the structure of Aucoin's theory of public management policy.

THE ELEMENTS OF THE ARGUMENT

Stated abstractly, Aucoin's theory of public management policy is a set of claims supported by warrants. In other words, the claims of the theory *(T)* are drawn from some set of warrants or other considerations through a process of practical argumentation. This statement can be expressed symbolically as follows:

(1) $T = A\,(\bullet)$.

In this expression, *T* stands for the theory of public management policy (specifically, its claims), (•) is a placeholder for the theory's warrants or other considerations, and *A* denotes that the inferential relationship between claims and warrants involves practical argumentation. Let us now identify the elements of $A\,(\bullet)$.

Aucoin's choice of warrants is informed, but not determined, by the ideas that became influential in Westminster countries during the 1980s. In his widely cited earlier article, Aucoin (1990) argued that managerialism is a major component of NPM ideas. Aucoin characterized managerialist ideas in terms of Peters and Waterman's (1982) *In Search of Excellence.* By and large, the same specification is made in Aucoin's later book. However, instead of referring to Peters and Waterman's best-seller, Aucoin (1995) refers to an official study of "well-performing organizations" in the Canadian public service, written by Otto Brodtrick for the Office of the Auditor General of Canada. As noted earlier, the study's findings were summarized in terms of four key determinants of organizational performance: emphasis on people, participatory leadership, innovative work styles, and strong client orientation (169). The substance of Brodtrick's argument accords with theories in the field of management, as Aucoin observes:

> In several of its manifestations, managerialism can be regarded as the contemporary version of the "human relations" movement which, in its hey-day, sought to humanize the traditional scientific management approach. The four emphases of well-performing organizations are thus hardly novel to normative management theory. Nevertheless, they are necessary ingredients of improved public management if public service organizations are to tap their most essential resource, namely the people who work in them. (170)

On the grounds that Aucoin fully accepts Brodtrick's theory of well-performing organizations (WPO), let us include the term *WPO* as an element of *A* (•).[9]

Aucoin's earlier article also identified public choice as a major component of NPM; both public choice and agency theory are discussed in his book. Although Aucoin does not say so, public choice and principal-agent theory share membership in a larger category of theories referred to as the New Institutional Economics (NIE) (Rutherford 1994). NIE has been described as the intellectual basis of NPM (Boston 1991; Moctezuma Barragán and Roemer 1999), a point about which some debate has taken place (see Schick 1996). For these reasons, let us identify *NIE* as the second element of *A* (•).

The third element of *A* (•) is a recurring argument about government. This argument appears to have a hierarchical structure with two principles—responsible government and good government—at its apex. These principles are not analyzed abstractly as philosophical concepts. Rather, their meaning is fixed in terms of less abstract, institutional concepts. This way of proceeding is evident in the following statements, drawn from Aucoin's text.

(i) Responsible government is party government. (25)

(ii) Responsible government requires that the political executive be responsible for policy formulation and policy implementation and that ministers are accountable to Parliament for actions taken by government departments. (25, 45)

(iii) A career public service (independent of party politics) is essential to good government. (29, 81)

(iv) The value of a career public service, beyond the simple eradication of partisan patronage in public service staffing, is its capacity to add value to governance on the basis of knowledge applied to the management of the state. (69)

(v) Responsible government requires that the public service be subordinate to the political executive. (25, 81)

(vi) Hierarchy is a fundamental principle of government. (8)

(vii) Good government requires that government departments be subject to at least a minimum set of values and standards. (160)

All these statements are broadly consistent with what Hood (1994) refers to as Progressive Public Administration (PPA). For this reason, *PPA* is sensibly represented as a third element of *A* (•).[10] In this connection, let us consider a few more statements, again drawn from Aucoin:

(viii) Good government requires sustained political commitment to the application of objective knowledge in governance. (72)

(ix) Good government requires that the total budget be shaped in the direction of the government's priorities. (125)

(x) Good government requires expenditure discipline. (125)

These statements have a contemporary feel to them, but they echo the major themes of PPA in the United States as reflected in the campaigns for civil service reform, executive reorganization, and budget reform (Karl 1963). For this reason (viii) through (x) can reasonably be subsumed under PPA. Now, consider three more statements:

(xi) Good government requires line managers to assume substantial responsibility for resource use. (127)

(xii) Executive fragmentation and administrative centralization have hamstrung both political leaders and public administrators, while failing to promote either policy coherence or expenditure discipline. (108, 111).

(xiii) Political conviction is the force that drives change in the management of the state. (68)

These three statements can be thought of as lessons learned (or at least fully accepted) during the past two decades of public administration in Westminster countries. As lessons from history, they are similar to the propositions grouped together under the heading PPA. If PPA is taken to be a living rather than extinct body of thought, statements (xi) through (xiii) can sensibly be considered revisions to the historical version of Progressive Public Administration (ΔPPA). For ease of exposition, let us define PPA as the union of historical PPA and ΔPPA. In other words, PPA refers to statements (i) to (xiii) collectively.

The main outlines of Aucoin's argument can thus be described as follows:

(2) $T = A\,(PPA, NIE, WPO)$

Now that we have a handle on the broad outlines of Aucoin's argument, our attention can focus on its more detailed specification.

THE ARGUMENT'S INTERNAL STRUCTURE AND FLOW

Aucoin's procedure for specifying NIE is to throw public choice and principal-agent theory into a scientific contest.[11] Public choice theory loses out on empirical grounds. Summarizing, Aucoin states:

> The exercise of bureaucratic power *per se* is first and foremost a function of delegated authority: bureaucrats do the bidding of their ministers.... If political leaders are not able to provide clear policy direction and ministerial leadership, the policies pursued will often be those formulated by public servants. The result, in these cases, is that public servants, rather than ministers, will appear to be in charge of government. More often than not, where public servants exercise considerable influence in the design and implementation of public policy, it is as a consequence of the political leadership devolving discretion to them. (36–37)[12]

According to Aucoin, principal-agent theory, by contrast, coheres with what is known about executive government:

> In several respects, agency theory is more useful than public choice theory in understanding ministerial-public service relations. While ministers and their public servants function in a formal structure with prescribed superior-subordinate

> status, the nature of this hierarchical arrangement masks an important reality. Ministers possess constitutional executive authority, but in the performance of their executive functions they depend on their subordinate officials for policy advice and administrative assistance for the two reasons that give rise to all "principal-agent" problems: limits on the time a principal can devote to making decisions, and the principal's lack of expertise on the matters for which decisions are required.... Relationships between ministers and their public servants are thus essentially relationships between principals and agents. (35)

The conclusion of this round of Aucoin's discussion is that principal-agent theory, but no other strand of NIE, should be considered in developing the theory of public management policy. However, the rationale for using principal-agent theory as a basis for Aucoin's theory of public management policy could have been expressed more precisely. Consider the following alternative presentation:

> For several reasons, the relationship between ministers and public servants can be described as a principal-agent relationship. First, in some principal-agent models, principals are unable to review agents' decisions because of a chosen decision structure (Breton 1996). This latter definitional assumption matches the empirical reality of the decision structure in government departments, characterized by extensive delegation from ministers to public servants.[13] Second, principal-agent models are based on the assumption that agents' decisions affect their principals' utility. In government, decisions made by public servants affect how well ministers perform their duties of office. Provided we substitute the concept of

> *duties* for that of *utility*, we can say that this second definitional assumption of agency theory matches facts about executive government. Third, principal-agent models are based on the assumption that the interests of principals and agents are not identical. That the interests of ministers are not the same as those of public servants is a reasonable inference from empirical research on government. This approximate match between agency models and empirical properties of government inclines us toward the view that minister–public servant relationships are principal-agent relationships.
>
> The definitional assumptions of principal-agent models imply that principals have to solve an agency problem.[14] What is true about principal-agent relations presumably applies to minister–public servant relations, for the reasons indicated earlier in this chapter. On this basis, we should presume that ministers have an agency problem to solve.

Presented in this fashion, Aucoin's statement that "relationships between ministers and their public servants are essentially relationships between principals and agents" is clear. Ministers can be described as having to solve an agency problem by virtue of three intersecting properties of their situation: their duties as ministers, decision structures that devolve authority to public servants, and some degree of conflict between the interests of ministers and public servants.

The next step in this argument is to draw inferences from principal-agent theory about how ministers should solve their agency problem. To draw such inferences, it is important to understand agency theory in its own terms. In agency theory, principals and agents are utility-maximizing individuals. By construction, the problem facing principals is how to exercise indirect control over agents' actions in order to maximize their own utility. By assumption, agents' actions can be controlled indirectly by incentives. It follows that rational principals use incentives to steer agents' actions. Incentives are modeled as mathematical functions relating rewards (dependent variables) to states of the world (independent variables) known as "outputs." This term can refer to any state of the world except for agents' actions. The function relating rewards to outputs is called an "incentive contract." Rational principals thus offer "incentive contracts" that reward agents on the basis of "outputs."

If ministers are principals, they should presumably solve their agency problem by rewarding the public service on the basis of outputs. Aucoin, however, does not conclude that the public service should be provided with incentive contracts. Instead, he points to a related but different solution to the agency problem within executive government. This solution is to develop "explicit contracts or agreements" about outputs (174). Discerning how this solution relates to the one that emerges from agency theory requires some work.

A HOLE IN AUCOIN'S ARGUMENT

Aucoin's presentation left out a crucial step in the reasoning process that involves overriding the normal implications of agency theory while preserving the idea that contracts are the solution to the problem faced by principals. If this step had been explicitly stated, we would immediately grasp two points. First, the concept of *explicit contract* in Aucoin's theory of public management policy is not equivalent to the concept of *contract* in agency theory. The explicit contracts that Aucoin recommends are organizational performance plans in the usual sense of the term. A performance plan expresses authoritative aspirations for the results of an organization's activities within a given time frame. On the other hand, "explicit contract" within agency theory is a promise to reward an agent on the basis of a measured quantity called an output. Second, since explicit contracts are performance plans rather than schedules of rewards for agents, Aucoin needs to explain why the public service will be motivated to accomplish performance goals.

Aucoin's discussion implies that once authoritative aspirations are established, the public service will be motivated to satisfy them. While this presumption contradicts the defining assumptions of principal-agent models, it is nonetheless considered plausible within some other theories of human behavior in organizations. For instance, culture theory (Douglas 1990; Thompson, Ellis, and Wildavsky 1990; Hood 1998) suggests that authoritative aspirations influence individual behavior, provided that the cultural bias of the collectivity is hierarchist. In a hierarchist collectivity, members, following a logic of appropriateness, seek to satisfy role expectations (March and Olsen 1989). The high-group and high-grid properties of a hierarchist collectivity indicate that some combination of "social mechanisms" (Hedström and Swedberg 1998) are at work in the concrete situation to explain why members seek to satisfy authoritative aspirations for organizational results. By contrast, agency theory implicitly assumes that the cultural bias of the collectivity is individualist, that is, low-group and low-grid.[15] In agency theory, the social mechanism that is normally assumed to control agents' behavior is the opportunity to make choices that will lead to receiving a payoff that will satisfy the agent's desire for income.

Culture theory suggests that if executive government is a hierarchist collectivity, then presumably the public service is motivated to satisfy authoritative aspirations.[16] The remaining question is, why should we accept the presumption that executive government is a hierarchist collectivity? After all, much of the development of NIE-type theories of public bureaucracy has proceeded on the standard individualist assumptions of economic theory. On this question, Aucoin's argument is silent.

As a way forward, let us accept the rebuttable presumption that executive government is a hierarchist collectivity. The social mechanisms operating in this sort of concrete situation are therefore presumed to provide a link between formulated authoritative aspirations for the results of organizational activity, as codified in performance plans, and the choices made by actors in the public service. For convenience, let us stipulate that PPA refers to this presumption as well as to the others listed earlier.[17] The issue for discussion, then, is how exactly does Aucoin integrate PPA and agency theory in arriving at his theory of public management policy, specifically in claiming that ministers should write explicit contracts for the public service's outputs?

The meaning of "explicit contracts" within Aucoin's theory of public management policy is drawn from both agency theory and PPA. Agency theory provides the concept of *output* in terms of which contracts are defined (as well as the term "contract"). Agency theory also provides a rationale for writing contracts as a solution to the agency problem facing ministers. PPA provides the presumption that authoritative aspirations for organizational performance have the potential to motivate public ser-

Principal-Agent Theory	Progressive Public Administration	Theory of Public Management Policy
Principal	Ministers	Ministers
Agent	Public service	Public service
Actions	Actions	Actions
Decision structure	Delegation	Delegation
Agency problem		Agency problem
Incentive contracts	Plans and budgets	Performance agreements
Outputs		Outputs
	Resource use	Resource use
Reward	Responsibility	Responsibility

Figure 3. Three Frames of Reference

vants to take the actions that satisfy the terms of the "explicit contract."

Semantically, the structure of this part of Aucoin's argument involves constructing a frame of reference for the theory of public management policy *(T)*. Some clarity might be gained by describing the flow of argument in terms of cognitive semantics (Lakoff and Johnson 1980; Lakoff 1987; Barzelay and Lakoff 1995; Lakoff 1996). *T* is, by definition, the target domain, whereas PPA and agency theory are the source domains for *T*. Knowledge of the target domain is structured in terms of both PPA and agency theory (see figure 3). A direct implication of the view that ministers are principals while public servants are agents, given agency theory, is that ministers should write incentive contracts for the public service. This implication is, however, overriden, since *explicit contracts* as defined in Aucoin are not the incentive contracts as defined in agency theory. Explicit contracts, we recall, are authoritative aspirations for organizational effort. In this respect, Aucoin grants PPA priority over agency theory. On the other hand, agency theory provides the idea of formulating performance goals in terms of outputs. The concept of output in Aucoin's theory of public management policy comes directly from the conceptual schema of agency theory. This idea is not found in PPA. In agency theory, output means whatever the principals and agents agree upon as basis for rewarding the agents. Consistent with this usage, the meaning of *output* within the theory of public management policy is open to a virtually unlimited range of specifications.

In sum, Aucoin's theoretical claims about performance contracts are based on a synthesis of agency theory and PPA rather than on the former alone. This point and the flow of argumentation to which it refers, however, is essentially absent from the author's presentation. In this respect, the presentation inhibits critical discussion of Aucoin's theory of public management policy and misses an opportunity to stimulate policy dialogue about the New Public Management.

FROM THEORY TO EVALUATION

The theory of public management policy is part of a compound argument. A second round of argument is the evaluation of public management policies in the Westminster context during the period of Aucoin's study. The broad outline of this unit of argument is as follows:

(3) $E = A\,(S, T)$,

where *E* stands for evaluative claims about specific public management policies, *S* stands for a survey of policy choices,[18] and *T* refers to the theory of public management policy.

The basis for evaluative claims appears to be as follows. A policy *p* receives a positive evaluation when three conditions are jointly satisfied. The first is that *p* is practiced in at least one of the surveyed countries. The second is that the survey detects a satisfactory official rationale for *p*. The third is that *p* is consistent with *T*. Consistency can be interpreted in two ways. One is that principles of PPA are not violated. A prima facie violation would be a case where *p* reduces ministers' accountability to parliament for government departments. The second interpretation is that *p* satisfies the requirements for good government expressed as *T*. Prima facie evidence that such requirements are satisfied is that "performance contracting" occurs and that the determinants of well-performing organizations are fulfilled. The most important point to notice is that any observed *p* has to satisfy *T* in order to receive a positive evaluation.

The policy that receives an extremely favorable evaluation by Aucoin is the assignment of operational and policy responsibilities to different units within the hierarchical structure of executive government. This policy is exemplified in the United Kingdom by the decision to establish executive agencies within government departments; it is exemplified in New Zealand by the way ministerial portfolios were reorganized in the mid-1980s. The survey shows that this policy has a satisfactory official rationale. However, the question is how organizing around policy and operational responsibilities is backed by *T*.

A close reading of Aucoin's text indicates that *T* does not provide direct backing for this evaluation. PPA is concerned with broad institutional issues but not with the specific organizing principles of government departments and bureaus. Both WPO and agency theory are concerned with the process of management but not with the structure of organizations. Schools of thought that deal directly with organizational structure—including management accounting and control—are not among *T*'s warrants. What, then, is the basis for Aucoin's favorable evaluation of the executive agencies–type structure?

One clue is provided by Aucoin's statement that "the crucial advantage for good government is its requirement that ministers contract with chief executives for the delivery of specific outputs or services" (142). This statement suggests that backing is provided by the claim that performance contracting is generally a desirable approach, as a way for ministers to solve the agency problem. A second clue about how Aucoin draws a favorable evaluative inference about the policy/operations split is provided by the statement that "a greater degree of organizational differentiation for operational units can promote greater devolution for managerial effectiveness" (151). However, the term *managerial effectiveness* may refer to greater efficiency in the use of resources. If so, the argument entails a number of steps. The first is that "good government requires line managers to assume substantial responsibility for resource use" (127). This statement was inherited by *T* from the update to PPA, specifically, statement (x). The second is that modifying the organizational structure of government is conducive to managers assuming such responsibility. The third is that the separation of policy from operations is the sort of organizational structure that selectively decentralizes responsibility for resource decisions along the vertical axis of government and its component units. The evidence supporting these last two steps comes from the survey, although Aucoin himself notes that this evidence is not strong.

The mention of *managerial effectiveness* in the previous paragraph might also refer to determinants of well-performing organizations (see page 177). If so, the argument seems to be that WPO provides a rationale for separating policy from operations. This argument is necessarily indirect, since emphasis on people, participatory leadership, innovative work styles, and client orientation do not refer specifically to organizational structure. The fine structure of the argument that WPO provides backing to the evaluation is not altogether clear from the text (see page 177). Presumably, the argument is that professional managers are more likely than mandarins to practice the doctrines of WPO.

All told, the argument for separating policy and operations is complex and contingent. The rationale for the policy is that it has been accompanied by changes whose combined effect is to raise the odds that ministers will try to solve their agency problem through explicit contracts, that line managers will become more responsible for the efficient use of resources, and that operational organizations in government will be led by people who practice WPO. Given that many governments come to believe that establishing agencies per se is good practice, it is important to underscore the complexity and contingency of the argument for the policy/operations separation.

THEORETICAL STANDARDS AND PRACTICAL GUIDELINES FOR NPM ARGUMENTATION

Aucoin's book is at once a hopeful and a cautionary tale for scholars who wish to undertake broad-gauged arguments about NPM. This tale demonstrates the need to follow codified practices of practical argumentation. Attempts to codify these practices date back to Aristotle's discussion of deliberative rationality (Toulmin and Jonsen 1988). Revived by Toulmin's *Uses of Argument* (1958), scholarly discussion of deliberative rationality and practical argument entered contemporary policy and administrative studies with such works as Vickers (1965), Thompson (1987), and Majone (1989). This body of thought figures prominently in recent statements about public policy analysis (Dunn 1994), public management (Moore 1995), and social science generally (Lindblom 1990).

Argumentation theory provides general standards that apply to discussions of New Public Management. One standard is that every participant "must be willing to discuss his viewpoints and to formulate his point of view as clearly as possible in order that it might be open to critical discussion" (Walton 1992, 91). Participants express themselves in such a way that others can discern and appraise their arguments. This standard of practice is a tall order when participants belong to separate academic or professional disciplines.

A second standard is that participants be willing to accept, on a provisional basis, presumptions to which other participants (but not themselves) are partisan. When this proviso is not satisfied, the argumentation process will grind to a predictable halt. A third standard is that participants cooperate in evaluating inferences drawn from such presumptions. This standard reflects the view that inferences are not logically entailed by presumptions. Any given presumption may be judged of limited relevance to the what-to-do question at hand. To illustrate, participants might be inclined to challenge inferences about how to motivate public servants drawn from generalizations about firms on the grounds that the same rules are likely to produce different effects in the two contexts.[19] Accordingly, a third standard of argumentation is that participants should cooperate in critically discussing the plausibility of inferences.

The analysis of Aucoin's argument in light of argumentation theory suggests a number of specific guidelines for arguing about NPM. These guidelines are organized around the general form of a practical argument, $C = A(\bullet)$, where C refers to claims (or conclusions) and $A(\bullet)$ is the rationale for C. The discussion will begin with claims and then address the other aspects of an argument.

I. Discuss the claims

A. Indicate subject of the claims

NPM is a catch-all term, one reason why writings on the subject, taken together, are amorphous. Where appropriate, a writer should identify a specific subject: eligible subject categories are public management policy, executive leadership in government, program design and administrative structure, and government operations.

Illustration: the claims in Aucoin's book refer primarily to public management policy.

B. Indicate scope of the claims

Under scope, a major distinction is between universal and more limited claims. In limiting the scope of claims, a writer can refer to types of governmental systems, cultures, policy domains, and time frames.

Illustration: The scope of Aucoin's doctrinal claims about public management policy is limited to Westminster systems. These claims refer to an indefinite time horizon; in this respect, they are meant to be broad in application.

C. Indicate nature of the claims

A major distinction is between theory and policy arguments as defined earlier in this chapter. Recall that both terms refer to practical arguments. In the case of theory, the claims are doctrines. In the case of policy arguments, the claims are evaluations or proposals.

Illustration: Aucoin's text includes doctrines, evaluations, and proposals.

D. Match claims to units of argument

Some discussions of NPM are networks or systems of arguments, which are usefully labeled "compound arguments." Each major unit of argument within a compound argument requires a specific discussion of its claims.

Illustration: The major units of Aucoin's compound argument include a theory of public management policy applicable to Westminster systems *(T);* an evaluation of public management policies in the United Kingdom, New Zealand, and Australia *(E);* and proposals for public management policy change in Canada *(P)*. These units of argument deal with the same subject, public management policy. The spatial scope of claims about *T* is Westminster systems, whereas the spatial scope of *P* is Canada. The temporal scope of *T* is indefinite, whereas the temporal scope of *P* is relatively near term.

E. Introduce substance of key claims

This step is to provide an initial description of the claims. It is useful to indicate if the claim is to be qualified or significantly elaborated at a later stage.

Illustration: Aucoin claims that "improving public management...requires that managers, as agents, have explicit contracts or performance agreements with their ministers, or superiors, as their principals" (174). It would be useful to indicate where in the discussion explicit contracts and performance agreements will be defined and contrasted with contracts in agency theory.

II. Discuss the warrants and presumptions

A. Identify source domains

The elements of *A* (•) are the "source domains" that provide the presumptions and warrants for the argument. In the interest of facilitating comparison among works in the field, the elements of *A* (•) should be broadly described.

Illustration: Aucoin's discussion of *T* can be described as follows:

(4) $T = A\,(PPA, NIE, MAN)$,

where PPA refers to Progressive Public Administration, NIE refers to the New Institutional Economics, and MAN refers to schools of thought about management. We can notice immediately from the inclusion of PPA in *A* (•) that Aucoin's argument is different from discussions that consider only NIE and/or MAN.

B. Indicate relations among elements of compound arguments

In the case of compound arguments, the claims of one unit of argument are the elements of *A* (•) in another unit. In this case, it is more important to indicate precise linkages among units of argument than to identify elements of *A* (•) in broad terms.

Illustration: In Aucoin's book,

(5) $E = A\,(S, T)$,

where *E* is the conclusion of his evaluation of public management policies in the United Kingdom, Australia, and New Zealand, *S* refers to his survey of practice in these countries, and *T* is the conclusion of his argument on the theory of public management policy. In the next round of argument, the conclusion/claim in (5) becomes a warrant for policy proposals in Canada. Symbolically, *E* moves from the left-hand side of (5) to the right-hand side of (6):

(6) $P = A\,(S, E)$,

where *P* refers to policy proposals for Canada, *S* refers to his in-depth survey of practice in Canada and *E* is the conclusion of his evaluation of public management policies in the other Westminster countries.

C. Specify the terms

Specification is needed when the argument selects from the broad categories of ideas that define the NPM field of discussion.

Illustration: Aucoin selects agency theory (T_{PA}) from New Institutional Economics (*NIE*), and he selects the theory of well-performing organizations (*WPO*) from managerial schools of thought (*MAN*):

(7) $NIE = T_{PA}$

(8) $MAN = WPO$

A rationale should be provided for the selection made.

Illustration: Aucoin's rationale for expression (7) is that public choice theory is inconsistent with empirical political science, whereas principal-agent theory encapsulates what is known about the minister–public service relationship.

Specification is needed when the terms are ambiguous.

Illustration: agency theory is "ambiguous" in the sense that different models emphasize different assumptions. Aucoin could have pointed to specific agency models that emphasize delegation as a decision structure. Ambiguity about the term *PPA* is perhaps best minimized by listing statements that characterize this position.

III. Explicate the informal logic

The term *informal logic* refers to how claims are supported by warrants and how conclusions are reached through presumptive reasoning (Walton 1992). Explicating the informal logic of a practical argument is analogous to presenting the logical steps by which a result is derived from a set of axiomatic assumptions. The most suitable guidance here is to underscore the goal, namely to "formulate [a] point of view as clearly as possible in order that it might be open to critical discussion" (Walton 1992, 91). This performance standard can be expressed in terms of specific principles for addressing scholarly readers.

A. Formalize the argument

When the relationship between claims and warrants can be readily and crisply described, it is useful to do so. Formalizing the argument allows readers to redirect their effort from identifying the argument's structure to considering the argument's substance. For instance, formalizing the argument makes it easier to inventory topics for critical discussion.

Illustration: The structure of the argument represented by expression (5) might be described as follows:

E refers to the set of public management policies *(P)* that qualify as good practice. A given policy *p* is deemed good practice whenever it jointly satisfies the following conditions. First, *p* is observed in at least one of the surveyed countries. Second, *p* has a

> satisfactory official rationale. Third, p is coherent with the theory of public management policy *(T)*.[20]

Aucoin's point would come through powerfully: neither theory nor observed practice is sufficient on its own to warrant claims about good practice. The reader's attention could then focus on the approach and its use by the author. Eligible topics include the adequacy of the category scheme in terms of which p is defined and the method for judging whether any given p is "coherent" with T.

B. Convey the experience of a discussion

When claims are arrived at through a sequence of inferential steps within a unit of argument, an author could present the argument as if reporting on how a conversation progressed from an initial point to a conclusion.

> Illustration: Aucoin would have followed this guideline if he had written: "Ministers are principals and public servants are agents. An implication is that ministers have an agency problem on their hands. This implication is plausible because it coheres with empirical knowledge obtained through 'behavioral' research in political science. A further implication, based on agency theory, is that ministers should provide public servants with incentive contracts. This inference is rejected here because it is based on the unacceptable presumption that the cultural bias of the public service is, or should be, individualist. Solutions to agency problems in government should be coherent with a hierarchist cultural bias. This stipulation leads to a

consideration of how 'explicit contracts' as authoritative, shared aspirations for efforts undertaken by the public service could function as a solution to the agency problem faced by ministers."

C. Take semantics seriously

An important link between *C* and *A* (•) is semantic. More specifically, the conceptual meaning of terms used to describe *C* is normally related to that of terms used to describe the elements of *A* (•). To understand the rationale for *C*, it may be necessary to know how *C*'s frame of reference is related to that of each element of *A* (•).

Illustration: A statement about *C* in Aucoin's theory of public management policy is, "improving public management... requires that managers, as agents, have explicit contracts or performance agreements with their ministers, or superiors, as their principals" (174). It should be made clear that the frame of reference of *C* is not agency theory. However, the concept of "output" within *C*'s frame of reference draws its meaning, in part, from agency theory.[21]

IV. Place the argument in context

The significance of the argument depends on how it relates to the rest of the literature on NPM in terms of method and substance. Placing the argument in this context is essential.

Illustration: Aucoin sought to differentiate his approach from the post-bureaucratic paradigm (Barzelay 1992).

In conclusion, practical argumentation is a well-developed scholarly practice in fields closely related to public management, including administrative law, political and professional ethics, and public policy analysis. This practice requires that arguments be stated as clearly as possible in order that they can be discussed critically (Walton 1992). Additional standards relate to the scrutiny of inferences drawn from such presumptions. Policy dialogue on NPM will be more fruitful when these standards are routinely practiced by scholarly commentators.

CHAPTER FIVE

Controversy and Cumulation in NPM Argumentation

Aucoin's evaluation of public management policies in the United Kingdom, Australia, and New Zealand is highly favorable. But this is not a judgment universally shared by academic specialists in public administration. Much of the controversy surrounds the New Zealand case, especially its emphasis on securing accountability for outputs—one of its main attractions from Aucoin's point of view. For instance, Robert Gregory (1995) doubts that a focus on outputs is suitable for most types of government programs. Allen Schick (1996), in a study commissioned by the New Zealand government, argues that securing output accountability should be balanced with management processes oriented toward achieving policy outcomes. These same concerns about output accountability are often echoed in professional discussions about the New Public Management, as well as in the policy-making process itself.

Sorting out the controversy about output accountability is a way to contribute to policy dialogue about the New Public Management. A major focus of the present chapter, then, is to identify the theoretical underpinnings of divergent evaluations of public management policies. For example, Gregory's critique is backed by James Q. Wilson's research on public bureaucracy, whereas Schick's argument is laced with ideas drawn from two fields of management, namely strategic management and management accounting and control. Aucoin's theoretical position on public management policy, as we have already seen, is built mainly on a synthesis of ideas from Progressive Public Administration (PPA) and principal-agent theory.

Understanding why authors reach different conclusions requires a close examination—and comparison—of their arguments. This process also provides an opportunity for cross-fertilization. For instance, Wilson's concept of outcome can usefully be incorporated into Aucoin's theory of public management policy, while Aucoin's concept of output (borrowed from agency theory) can usefully be incorporated into Wilson's conceptual framework. The result is a measurable step forward in argumentation about NPM.

Establishing a dialogue among authors who evaluate public management policies is useful, whether the result is to clarify differences or to achieve a synthesis. The final part of this chapter attempts to underscore this view about how to advance scholarly argumentation on NPM by applying it to my earlier book on the subject, *Breaking Through Bureaucracy* (1992).

GREGORY: RETRIEVING CONTINGENCY THEORY

The focus of Gregory's (1995) essay is the use of agency theory in shaping public management policies and managing government departments. Among other points, Gregory claims that the New Zealand model of public management encourages "all public agencies to treat all their tasks as if they were or could be made into production ones...an aspiration [which] seems insufficiently sensitive to differences among the sorts of tasks that public organizations are required to carry out" (58). This claim is backed by warrants drawn from James Q. Wilson's celebrated book, *Bureaucracy* (1989).[1] Wilson uses theoretical categories and illustrative examples to argue that the operating conditions of bureaus vary radically within government. Wilson's theory suggests that the effects of any given set of administrative systems or any given course of executive actions differ according to the bureau's specific operating conditions. In sum, situations within government are so radically different from one another that any one-size-fits-all approach to public management is bound to be misguided.

Wilson's Typology

Wilson identifies four types of situations, defined in terms of their specific operating conditions. These conditions are conceived in terms of the "observability" of outputs and outcomes. The meaning of *output* in Wilson's frame of reference is different from the meaning of this term in agency theory. Wilson defines output as a performed task. When Wilson says that outputs are observable, he appears to mean that two conditions are jointly satisfied. First, operators' work effort is programmed by the bureau's technostructure. Second, operators are literally supervised by managers. In other words, outputs are observable when a bureau is a machine bureaucracy as defined in Mintzberg's (1983)

		Outcomes	
		Observable	**Unobservable**
Outputs	**Observable**	Production	Procedural
	Unobservable	Craft	Coping

Figure 4. Wilson's Typology of Organizations

theory of organizational structure. The opposite case, where outputs are unobservable, obtains when operators' work is not programmed or when operators are not directly observed by managers.

The meaning of *outcome* comes from political science and policy studies. It refers to the goals of the programs operated by bureaus or, equivalently, the bureau's mandate. An outcome is unobservable when either of two conditions obtains. One is that judgments about organizational effectiveness are hampered by ambiguity about what is the agency's mandate. The other is that such judgments are hampered by uncertainty about the impact of programmatic actions (i.e., bureau efforts) on targeted problems. In other words, outcomes are unobservable when the effect of a bureau's work is known with a substantial time lag, if at all (Wilson 1989, 163).

Wilson's two-by-two matrix of situational types elaborates his general argument that public bureaucracy is not a monolithic phenomenon (see figure 4). The term *production organization* refers to a case where both outputs and outcomes are observable. The term *coping organization* refers to its diametric opposite where neither outputs nor outcomes are observable. Intermediate cases are termed *procedural organization* and *craft organization.* In the former, outputs are observable but outcomes are not; in the latter, outputs are not observable, but outcomes are. If "management" is securing compliance with standards—for example, standard operating procedures or agency mandates—then "management" in one type of organization is substantially different from management in another type—indeed, radically different between production and coping organizations.

The same analytic construct addresses the question of how public management and private management are different. The differences are most stark in the case of a coping organization, where outputs and outcomes are both unobservable. In a production organization, operating conditions are similar to a stereotypical case of private management. In this case, the task performance of operators is easily observed because their work is programmed and they are directly supervised. A production organization's performance can furthermore be evaluated as if it had a bottom line. In the two intermediate cases, public management bears some, if limited, resemblance to private management: in procedural organizations, the bureau-operator relationship is stereotypical insofar as work is programmed and operators are directly supervised, while the performance of a craft organization in relation to its mandate can be evaluated in an operationally relevant time frame.

Wilson's framework is awkward as a basis for critiquing agency-theoretic approaches to public management policy. Gregory's claim that agency theory encourages governments to manage all agencies as production organizations is surprising, since the defining assumptions of agency theory are that efforts—a concept that corresponds to Wilson's concept of output—are unobservable. The defining assumptions of agency theory models correspond more closely to the craft organization in Wilson's typology than to the production organization.

Going Forward on the Basis of Wilson's Theory

Gregory's effort to develop a theory of public management policy on the basis of Wilson's contingency approach is worth pursuing.[2] Suppose the specific task is to establish a dialogue with theories of public management policy based on agency theory—like Aucoin's. This task, however, is fraught with conceptual difficulties. For instance, in Wilson's frame of reference, *output* refers to the relationship between bureaus and operators, whereas *output* in Aucoin's theory refers instead to the relationship between overseers and bureaus. Wilson discusses the overseer-bureau relationship in terms of *outcomes*, suggesting that *outcome* in Wilson's frame of reference may be equivalent to *output* in Aucoin's theory. However, Aucoin's concept of *output* has no equivalent in Wilson's theory, while Wilson's concept of *outcome* has no equivalent in Aucoin's theory.[3]

In view of such conceptual difficulties, the effort should begin by outlining Wilson's overall framework within which the fourfold typology of organizations is nested. This framework can be analyzed by listing statements that describe Wilson's theory of executive government. These statements reveal the conceptual system (Lakoff and Johnson 1980) in terms of which Wilson analyzes government:

Bureaus perform *core tasks.*
Core tasks are defined by the *bureau's mandate.*
Mandates call for *outcomes.*
Constraints facing *bureaus* are *contextual goals.*
Overseers establish *mandates* and *contextual goals.*
Bureaus are supposed to *comply* with *mandates* and *contextual goals.*

Operators perform the *bureau's tasks.*
Outputs are *completed tasks.*
Operators are supposed to *comply* with *tasks.*

Work may be *programmed* or *unprogrammed.*
Operators and their *work* may or may not be directly *monitored.*

Outputs are *observable* when work is *programmed* and *operators* are directly *monitored* by managers.
Outcomes are *observable* when *compliance* with the *mandate* is known.
The *observability* of *outputs* and *outcomes* affects the *management process* in government.

As can be seen, Wilson's theory focuses on two compliance relationships, namely between *(a)* overseers and bureaus and *(b)* bureaus and operators. Wilson's analytic description of the overseer-bureau agency relationship is usefully compared with Aucoin's description of minister–public service relationships. Comparison is aided by a consideration of the agency-theoretic distinction between decision and information structures (Breton 1996, 150).

Both Wilson and Aucoin describe the overseer-bureau relationship in terms of the decision structure of government: overseers delegate decisions to bureaus.[4] As modeled, overseer-bureau relations do not vary within government in terms of their decision structure. Differences between Wilson and Aucoin arise in describing the information structure of government. Wilson implicitly introduces the concept of information structure in his discussion of "outcomes." In Wilson's terms, "outcomes are unobservable" when the effects of a government program on the achievement of programmatic goals are known only after a substantial passage of time (or are never known). This idea comes from knowledge about the policy implementation process.[5] Translated into agency theory terms, the idea that "outcomes are unobservable" means that the "payoffs" of a bureau's efforts are revealed—if ever—in a future period, for example, after agents have been rewarded for their efforts. This information structure, where "payoffs" are revealed outside an operationally relevant time frame, obtains in procedural and coping organizations but not in production and craft organizations.

The contingency situation where program effects are revealed with a substantial time lag is an important feature of Wilson's model of overseer-bureau relationships, but is absent from Aucoin's theoretical argument.[6] Aucoin's argument is based on PPA, well-performing organizations (WPO), and agency theory, none of which incorporates models of policy implementation. Although the lag structure of policy effects can be modeled in agency terms, Aucoin's use of agency theory does not extend that far. On this count, Wilson's model of overseer-bureau relations is arguably better than Aucoin's model of minister–public service relations.

In other ways, Aucoin's description of the minister–public service relationship is arguably better than Wilson's. In Wilson's discussion, a bureau's tasks are related to its mandate. However, the way a mandate is translated into tasks is not much discussed because his attention focuses on the process of securing operators' compliance with given tasks. The selection of tasks seems to be conceived as a managerial function that occurs within the policy implementation process. In this respect, the conceptual structure of Wilson's theory reflects the view that policy-making and policy implementation are (or should be) activities temporally separated within government. By contrast, Aucoin repudiates the related idea that policy and administration must be dissociated to achieve good government. Indeed, his use of agency theory supports his clear argument that policy-making, policy implementation, and administration should be integrated through performance contracting (Aucoin 1995, 178).

In sum, developing a synthesis of Wilson's and Aucoin's theories is a way to address the controversy raised by Gregory and to achieve modest progress in scholarly argumentation about the New Public Management. Wilson's theory shows that a theory of public management policy needs to take into account the information structure of the policy implementation process. Aucoin, for his part, goes further than Wilson in envisioning a constructive integration of policy-making and administration. A synthesis would state that an agency problem in government always arises in one of two forms. One form of the agency problem arises when the programmatic effects of the public service's efforts are known within an operationally relevant time frame, in other words, where outcomes are observable. The other form arises when these programmatic effects are delayed beyond an operationally relevant time frame, in other words, where outcomes are unobservable. Common to these two forms of the agency problem in government is the delegation of decisions to the public service. If the precise form of the agency problem is different depending on the observability of outcome, then it stands to reason that the solution to this problem varies as well. Accordingly, public management policies should be evaluated in part on the basis of whether they allow the method of performance contracting to be matched to the specific type of agency problem arising in government.

What Gregory Might Have Written

If Gregory had engaged both Aucoin's and Wilson's discussions and if he followed the practice of argumentation as proposed by Walton (1992), he might have written his essay in the following way:

> In a recent book, Peter Aucoin put forth a theory of public management policy as a basis for evaluating New Zealand's and other experiences with NPM. An element of this argument is agency theory. Personally, I do not favor principal-agent theory as a basis for reasoning about public management, and I am troubled by the practice of performance contracting in my country.
>
> The perspective I take on public management is much like James Q. Wilson's. Wilson's theory is appealing because it is rooted in what operators do to perform a bureau's tasks, yet it also speaks to the realities of vague mandates, intrusive

constraints, and the dynamics of policy implementation in public management. Wilson's theory of bureaucracy is highly attuned to differences among situations. The same cannot be said for Peter Aucoin's theory. Aucoin's presumptions and inferences presuppose that the public service is homogeneous; James Q. Wilson has argued convincingly the opposite.

With Wilson's approach in mind, I would like to raise concerns about Aucoin's doctrine that political executives should contract for output. If the public service's responsibility is defined exclusively in terms of agreed outputs, then public servants will not be responsible for programmatic impact. This situation could be detrimental to achieving public policy goals. For this reason, I am disinclined to accept Aucoin's theoretical argument on this point. Accordingly, I question his favorable evaluation of New Zealand's reforms.

To keep the conversation moving forward, I would like to suggest that we agree on a contingency approach to performance contracting. Where outcomes are observable, Aucoin's theory is fairly plausible as far as it goes. Where outcomes are unobservable (in Wilson's sense), a qualification is definitely called for. I would propose attaching a proviso to the doctrine that "political executives should contract for output (in Aucoin's sense)." The proviso would read, "except when outcomes (in Wilson's sense) are unobservable, in which case a more balanced set of controls over a bureau is indicated."

ALLEN SCHICK'S SPIRIT OF REFORM

In the mid-1990s, two of New Zealand's central agencies commissioned Allen Schick to evaluate implemented public management policies in the central government. A prominent U.S.

scholar in public administration and management, Schick has made a career of studying budgetary and other public management reforms around the world. The report, entitled *The Spirit of Reform: Managing the New Zealand State Sector in a Time of Change* (1996), is a policy argument according to the definition laid out in the previous chapter. While both Schick and Aucoin express broadly favorable evaluations of the New Zealand case, Schick is much more critical. He is especially critical of government-wide institutional rules and routines affecting the planning and resourcing of government departments' activities. As both Schick and Aucoin are authorities on public management policy, scholars in public management need to understand why their evaluations differ.

As a method of analysis, let us assume that Schick's discussion of public management policy has the same general form as Aucoin's:

(1) $E = A(S, T)$,

where E stands for evaluative claims, S stands for a survey of practice, and T stands for a theory of public management policy. Differences in evaluative claims can presumably be traced to differences in survey evidence, differences in theories of public management policy, or differences in the way practical conclusions are drawn from survey evidence and theoretical claims.

Accounting for Divergence

The authors worked with different kinds of survey evidence. Schick's project involved interviews with over 100 respondents as well as a review of documents providing a wealth of information about New Zealand's public management policies as implemented. Schick was thus informed about the routines through which policy measures were put into practice. The focus of Aucoin's survey, by contrast, is on institutional rules.

Schick's implicit theory of public management policy is also different from Aucoin's. As we have seen, the outline of Aucoin's theory of public management policy is $T = A$ (*PPA, NIE, MAN*). Schick, by contrast, does not include the New Institutional Economics (NIE) among the sources of his theoretical views about public management policy, and he specifies management (MAN) differently than does Aucoin.[7] Whereas Aucoin specified MAN as four determinants of well-performing organizations (WPO), Schick implicitly specifies this same broad term as theories and doctrines of management accounting and control (MAC) and strategic management (SM). These specific terms refer to bodies of thought associated with disciplines within management: MAC is associated with the functional discipline of management control, and SM is associated with business policy.[8] Compared to Aucoin's, Schick's theory takes account of a wider range of professional thought about management.

Drawing Evaluative Inferences

Management accounting and control is a basis for Schick's criticism of New Zealand's government-wide routines for budgeting. One key criticism is that New Zealand's government departments have not developed adequate costing systems. Arraying information on planned expenditures by output is one matter; it is quite another to know what resources need to be consumed in the process of creating outputs. Schick argues that a "resourcing system" that includes budget information arrayed by output but that excludes good cost information is defective: in such a case, ministers and central agencies make resourcing decisions on a weak analytic basis. Although Schick does not discuss the design of costing systems in detail, he does indicate that MAC is a source of ideas about how to do so (see pages 67–69). In any event, Schick uses MAC to argue that the analytic basis for resourcing government departments in New Zealand is weaker that it should be.[9]

A combination of strategic management and PPA is a basis for Schick's criticisms of routines for managing the relationship among chief executives, central agencies, and ministers. These routines, in his view, were marked by an excessive concern for output accountability, especially in the period before New Zealand initiated a strategic planning process to identify desired "outcomes" for governmental activity over a medium term. Schick's version of PPA is closely associated with Charles Merriam, a prominent exponent of "planning" in government whose influence over the field of public administration was prodigious during the 1920s and 1930s (Karl 1963; Friedman 1987). In this version, government is viewed as a collective problem solver. To translate this functional view of government (Nelson 1996) into a theory of public management policy, Schick draws on ideas of strategic management:

> Strategic capacity is the capacity of the government or a department to anticipate and plan for future changes in its environment, recast its objectives and programmes accordingly, define and specify desired future outcomes, reallocate

> resources to achieve them, evaluate results, and measure progress. (53)

From this standpoint, New Zealand's public management policies had shortcomings at the time Schick wrote in 1996:

> The lack of attention to the question of strategic capacity was a serious flaw in the original design of the New Zealand reforms. This design flaw was not an oversight but derived from the strong emphasis on operational efficiency and accountability. . . . The New Zealand system still is geared more to short-term production of outputs than planning for the long haul, and to account for what has been produced than to evaluate progress in achieving major policy objectives. (53)

From this same standpoint, Schick praised New Zealand's maturing process for identifying "strategic results areas" (SRAs) at the governmental level and "key results areas" (KRAs) at the departmental level.[10]

Why Schick Is More Critical Than Aucoin

Schick's evaluation of New Zealand's public management policies is less favorable than Aucoin's for several reasons.[11] First, Schick's survey (S) is different from Aucoin's. Thanks to his firsthand examination, Schick surveyed public management policies—including their associated routines—in detail. Second, management accounting and control ideas (MAC) provide a different basis for evaluating public management policies than those drawn from agency theory, even when modified by PPA. In particular, MAC provides more guidance than agency theory does on how executives should control the processes of resource acquisition and utilization. This guidance includes the development of an analytic basis for knowing and evaluating the consumption of resources in productive activities. Such guidance, Schick argues, is fully relevant to ministers and central agencies, because "managing costs" is an inescapable responsibility whenever outputs are produced by government departments or when competition among providers is weak or nonexistent. Schick's crucial distinction between "contracting for outputs" and "managing costs" does not arise in Aucoin's theory of public management policy because the latter does not incorporate MAC.

Third, Schick and Aucoin specify PPA differently. The functional idea of government as a public problem solver —associated with progressive thought about "planning"—is an integral part of Schick's theory of public management policy.[12] While Schick's version of PPA is a functional view of good government, Aucoin's version emphasizes institutional requisites of good government. Schick's functional version of PPA, elaborated with ideas drawn from strategic management, is a basis for his attention to outcomes and his qualified assessment of New Zealand's output-oriented public management policies.

Finally, because of the influence of strategic management ideas, Schick conceives of public management policies as complements (Milgrom and Roberts 1995): the effects of any given institutional rule depend on the presence of certain others. For instance, the effects of rules that focus attention and responsibility on delivering outputs depend on the presence of strategic planning and costing systems. Schick's approach is not to evaluate public management policies one at a time, but as a system.

Thus, the divergent evaluations of Schick and Aucoin can be attributed largely to differences in their theories of public management policy.

Critiquing the Contractual Model

Schick's *Spirit of Reform* includes a critique of New Zealand's well-publicized "administrative philosophy" (Hood and Jackson 1991), which Schick labels "the contractual model of reform." Schick's complaint about this reform model is multifold. First, it places excessive emphasis on compliance and too little on improvement. Without being guided by this value, the contractual model of reform is not "managerialist" in orientation even though it allows for choices to be made.[13] Second, the contractual model of reform casts ministers in the role of "purchasers" even when government departments are the providers. Schick argues that the philosophy of casting ministers as purchasers—while it has its merits—distorts the resourcing process. In particular, New Zealand has not developed the costing systems that "owners"—but not "purchasers"—need. Without suitable costing information, departments are funded on a somewhat arbitrary basis, an alleged effect of which is to deplete government departments of the human capital and infrastructure they may need to respond adequately to future policy requirements. Third, the contractual model of reform is disconnected from a vision of government as a public problem solver. Schick drives home this point by arguing that the process of identifying outcomes (i.e., SRAs and KRAs) was a departure from—rather than an extension of—the contractual model of reform. For all these reasons, Schick would presumably criticize Aucoin's theory of public management policy for its inclusion of agency theory, for its narrow specification of management ideas, and for its institutionally oriented rather than functionally oriented version of PPA. [14]

A Focus for Debate

The comparative analysis of Schick's and Aucoin's discussions of public management policy indicates some degree of consensus and controversy on the New Public Management. A major point of consensus is that rigorous argumentation about this specific subject is desirable and feasible whether the conclusions are standing or action volitions. A point of dissent concerns the selection of warrants for a theory of public management policy. Aucoin's theory is a "contractual" approach, while Schick's is "managerial." This dichotomy may be a useful way to frame the debate over the theory of public management policy. However, labels should do no more than draw attention to a range of intellectual controversies on a given subject. This proviso should forcefully apply to any suggestion to contrast contractual and managerial theories of public management policy.

BREAKING THROUGH BUREAUCRACY REVISITED

The framework for analyzing arguments about public management policy developed in this book can also be usefully applied to my earlier *Breaking Through Bureaucracy*, which was published a few years before Aucoin's and Schick's studies. From the perspective of the present volume, *BTB* discusses two related types of claims. One analytically distinct discussion is of public management policies; the other is executive leadership of staff organizations. The main objects of the first discussion are government-wide institutional rules and organizational routines concerning procurement, staffing, general or auxiliary services, and information policy. The main object of the second discussion is "organizational interventions" from a position of executive authority.[15]

Evaluating Public Management Policy

One main line of argument of *BTB* is that the rules and routines put into place in Minnesota's staff agencies between 1984 and 1990 were a reasonable and effective response to the problems that executives and legislators sought to solve. That argument can be recast as an evaluation of aspects of Minnesota's public management policies circa 1990. The outlines of this argument can be described as follows:

(2) $E_M = A\,(S_M, T)$,

where S_M stands for the survey of implemented public management policies in Minnesota in the 1984–90 time frame and E_M stands for the evaluation of those same policies.

While the evaluation was evidently informed by general arguments about public management, the reasoning was not made as explicit as I now believe is appropriate for scholarly argumentation about this subject. In following the standards and guidelines proposed in the previous chapter, I would identify a theory of public management policy *(T)* and then discuss how the study's evaluative claims relate to it. An interpretation of my own argument is as follows:

(3) $T = A\ (PPA, MAN)$
$MAN = MAC, SM, WPO$

Readers familiar with *BTB* may be surprised at the inclusion of PPA in expression (3). The book portrayed the "post-bureaucratic paradigm" as antithetical to the "bureaucratic paradigm" and attributed the latter to the progressive reform movements. However, the post-bureaucratic paradigm is not antithetical to PPA if the latter is regarded as an evolving argument (a point I attribute to Aucoin) and if PPA is primarily specified in functional as opposed to institutional terms (as does Schick, in my interpretation). From this standpoint, PPA is an integral part of the sort of theory of public management policy that is implicit in both my 1992 book and Schick's 1996 study of the New Zealand reforms. If the term *paradigm* is translated into "theory of public management policy," then the distinguishing features of the post-bureaucratic paradigm (relative to the bureaucratic paradigm) are its functionally oriented specification of PPA and its inclusion of *(a)* ideas about management accounting and control in decentralized organizations, *(b)* ideas about the strategic management of organizations, and *(c)* ideas about high-performance organizations.

The role of PPA in my argument (as in Schick's) is to evaluate public management policies—government-wide institutional rules and the organizational routines of staff organizations—in terms of their impact on line agencies' ability to "comply with their mandates" (Wilson 1989). The primary role of management accounting and control (MAC) is to provide a basis for evaluating policies concerning the funding and control of general service activities such as data processing, telecommunications, office cleaning, records storage, usage of the motor vehicle fleet, printing, and typewriter repair. From this standpoint, the governance of the central data-processing and telecommunications service as a "utility" would be evaluated as a solution to a recurring issue of management control in decentralized organizations.[16] MAC is also a source of the broad argument that internal controls be evaluated on a benefit-cost basis. This line of argument is a basis for evaluating changes in the purchasing function, such as the devolution of authority to line agencies for small purchases. As for strategic management (SM), its primary role is to provide a basis for evaluating the routines utilized by Minnesota's Information Policy Office to judge whether expenditures on information systems were closely aligned with government departments' programmatic directions.

The primary role of WPO—the ideas Aucoin borrowed from Brodtrick—is to evaluate routines by which frontline employees in central staff organizations perform their tasks. The determinants of well-performing organizations include strong client orientation, innovative work styles, participatory leadership, and emphasis on people (Aucoin 1995, 169). WPO provides backing for a favorable evaluation of such policies as increasing the signature authority of frontline purchasing agents, inculcating a problem-solving orientation among frontline staffing officials, and placing a huge emphasis on customer service in the general services activities. A secondary role of WPO—specifically, the principle of a strong client orientation—is to provide backing for the doctrine of separating service from control, a cornerstone of the Minnesota Department of Administration's overall strategy and a rationale for its internal restructuring.

The chief advantage of such an exposition is to facilitate critical discussion of evaluative claims about the public management policies surveyed in Minnesota. The favorable evaluation of these policies could be criticized on the basis of whether *(a)* the theoretical basis of evaluation *(T)* is well chosen, *(b)* the survey *(S)* is well done, and *(c)* the evaluation is clearly related to *S* and *T*. With clearer exposition, controversy would be more likely to concern such matters of analysis and judgment.

Since the time when *Breaking Through Bureaucracy* was published, the literature on the New Public Management has matured. Public management scholars now have a frame of reference for describing with some precision the subject of the claims being discussed, as the distinction between public management policies and executive leadership illustrates. Clearly specified approaches to evaluating as well as designing public management policies are now available. In this sense, a foundation has been laid for scholars to make a contribution to the analysis and evaluation of public management policies.

CHAPTER SIX

CONCLUSION

New Public Management is a field of discussion largely about policy interventions within executive government. The characteristic instruments of such policy interventions are institutional rules and organizational routines affecting expenditure planning and financial management, civil service and labor relations, procurement, organization and methods, and audit and evaluation. These instruments exercise pervasive influence over many kinds of decisions made within government. While they do not determine the scope or programmatic content of governmental activity, these government-wide institutional rules and organizational routines affect how government agencies are managed, operated, and overseen: they structure that part of the governmental process usefully described as public management.[1] In recent years, political executives, central agency leaders, and legislators in numerous settings have demonstrated a sustained interest in policies affecting public management, the best-known cases of which are the United Kingdom, New Zealand, and Australia.

NPM AND ITS PROBLEMS

New Public Management (NPM) is concerned with the systematic analysis and management of public management policy. This policy domain relates to all government-wide, centrally managed institutional rules and routines affecting the public management process. For this reason, the domain encompasses multiple organizations within government, including central agencies responsible for budgeting, accounting, civil service and labor relations, efficiency and quality, auditing, and evaluation. Systematic analysis involves clear argumentation about the relationship between context, goals, policy instruments, and choices. Systematic management is a process of decision making that is both informed by analysis and well adapted to the political and organizational forces that shape decisions and their downstream effects. NPM as a field of discussion is thus rooted in that of systematic management and policy analysis.

NPM's Twin Elements

If NPM is a field of discussion about public management policy, it is important to be clear about its elements. This book proposes two main elements, which policy-makers need to consider if public management policy is to be placed on a sound footing. The first element focuses on the political and organizational processes through which policy change takes place. These processes are influenced by a host of conditions, both institutional (such as the overall structure of the governmental system and the specific organization of central administrative responsibilities) and noninstitutional (such as policy spillover and interference effects). Policy dynamics can be analyzed in terms of specific mechanisms and patterns through which policy-making processes operate. The key analytic issues linked to this element of NPM discussion include estimating the feasibility of policy change and crafting lines of action to satisfy the situation-specific requirements of policy entrepreneurship.

The focus of the second element is the substantive analysis of public management policy. This analysis concerns the advantages and disadvantages of various combinations of government-wide institutional rules and routines within specified contexts. Analysis is best regarded as a process of argumentation, for two reasons. First, policy conclusions—even retrospective, evaluative ones—are supported by beliefs about government that are plausible rather than definitively true. Second, analysis takes place in a dialectical context where disagreement arises because of the variety of beliefs, expertise, and interests that are relevant to the choice of management controls in government.

These broad categories—process and substance—give some structure to the abstract conception of NPM proposed here. Thinking of NPM in these terms helps to focus inquiry on each of two key issues of public policy analysis—feasibility and desirability—that are relevant for policy-makers. Focusing on these analytic issues also provides a more definitive context for discussing methods for conducting research and argumentation on public management policy. This conception of NPM is superior for learning from experience than was NPM's initial formulation.

NPM's Origins and Problems

To benefit fully from previous work on NPM, scholars and policy-makers need to be familiar with how this field of discussion has evolved. In sketching the evolution of the NPM discussion, it is useful to distinguish scholarship from both professional commentary and actual policy-making activity. Discussion taking place within governments—for example, those taking place within the New Zealand Treasury in the 1980s and presented in its postelection briefing, *Government Management*—will be referred to as NPM_1. Professional commentary—exemplified by Osborne and Gaebler's (1992) *Reinventing Government* and illustrated by publications of the OECD Public Management Service—is denoted by NPM_2. Finally, academic scholarship—the category to which nearly all works cited in the present volume belong—is referred to as NPM_3.

At the risk of oversimplification, I present the following account of NPM's evolution:

1. The concept of New Public Management originated in NPM_3 (Hood and Jackson 1991; Hood 1991).

2. NPM was initially characterized as an international trend. The essence of the trend was distilled from an array of specific ideas about management and government drawn from NPM_1 and NPM_2 (Hood 1991). An influential account identified two paradigms of ideas: public choice and managerialism (Aucoin 1990).

3. The main empirical referents of the trend were the United Kingdom, Australia, and New Zealand in the 1980s.

4. The case of New Zealand (NPM_1) acquired special significance in both NPM_2 and NPM_3 for two main reasons. First, policy change took place across a wide range of distinct areas—expenditure planning, financial management, organization, civil service, and labor relations—within a single three-

year parliamentary mandate (Boston et al. 1991). The New Zealand case thereby demonstrated even more clearly than the United Kingdom under Margaret Thatcher that public management had become a policy domain. Second, the New Zealand Treasury's deliberations and policy arguments were framed in terms of economic theories of organization and government. This style of argumentation was highly unconventional in public management policy-making. The conjuncture of rapid comprehensive change in public management policies and an unconventional pattern of argumentation made the New Zealand case (NPM_1) especially noteworthy. Numerous scholars commented (NPM_3) that economic theories of organization and government (New Institutional Economics) constituted the intellectual foundations of New Public Management.[2]

5. In professional and academic discussion, countries where public management policy change has been less than comprehensive were labeled as "laggards" (Aucoin 1995).

6. The notion that the NPM is a widely applicable blueprint for the organizational design of the public sector is commonplace in professional discussion (NPM_2).

7. Some scholars in continental Europe argue that NPM is an Anglo-American model whose relevance outside its core cases is highly questionable.[3]

While points 4 through 7 are all worrisome, the last two points evince the most severe present limitations of the NPM field of discussion. A blueprint approach to policy design is highly questionable: the functioning of a given system of formal arrangements, such as management controls, depends on the context in which it operates. On the other hand, the equation of

NPM with an Anglo-American approach to public management policy is hardly a recipe for policy analysis and learning on an international scale. While these two extreme views about NPM are equally unsatisfactory, they grow out of the history of this field of discourse. In particular, these limitations can be attributed to the initial conception of NPM as a trend, centered on three similar cases.

AN EMERGING POLICY APPROACH TO PUBLIC MANAGEMENT

If the NPM field of discourse is to be more useful for practitioners, a decisive turn away from its initial contours is required. Adopting a public policy approach to this subject constitutes such a turn. The policy approach directs attention toward explaining change in public management policy on a comparative basis; it would also place a high value on rigorously argued evaluative discussions of policy choices.

The policy approach can build on the accumulated strengths of the NPM_3 literature. As shown in chapter 2, scholars have explored policy-making episodes and sequences in a number of cases. This literature provides a starting point for explaining similarities and differences in public management policy change across cases. To accelerate research progress, it is advantageous to apply well-honed explanatory frameworks to such case evidence, as shown in chapter 3. Processual models of agenda setting and alternative generation explain, for instance, how ideas from economics and management contributed to policy change in the benchmark cases of NPM. Processual models also explain the effects of interventions in the policy-making process by executive authorities, such as prime ministers and top officers of central agencies.

A policy approach can build on the evaluative literature discussed in chapters 4 and 5 as well. These works provide commentary on policy choices, such as output budgets, accrual accounting systems, performance agreements with chief executives, and division of executive government into myriad single-purpose organizational units. This recent development moves beyond the initial conception of NPM as a trend by engaging in argumentation about the desirability of specific public management policies (institutional rules and organizational routines). Notably, this literature is yielding controversy over public management policies. For instance, Schick (1996) expresses strong reservations about specific aspects of New Zealand's institutional rules and organizational routines in the public management domain. In contrast, Aucoin (1995) offers few doubts about the desirability of public management policies in the United Kingdom, Australia, and New Zealand. The basis for such disagreements can be traced to the analytic frameworks employed. One major difference lies in the specific strands of managerial thought that the authors rely upon to evaluate public management practices.

The Policy Approach Exemplified

Schick's study of New Zealand's reforms serves as an exemplar of policy-oriented, academically rigorous analysis within the New Public Management. In analyzing policy choices, the study penetrates through the fog of NPM themes (such as an output orientation) and buzzwords (such as performance contracting).

The object of evaluation is the system of management controls—broadly defined—operating throughout the departments of government. These controls are described in terms of their routine—as opposed to hypothetical—operation. Moreover, the description of the system of controls illuminates how organizational factors—such as the cultures of central agencies—influence the evolving operationalization of public management policies at the level of routines and transactions.

The standpoint from which Schick evaluated the observed system of controls is another facet of the study deserving serious consideration by practitioners and scholars alike. By standpoint, I mean general ideas that serve as a plausible basis for evaluating or designing public management policies in particular settings.[4] The ideas are drawn from bodies of thought and knowledge related to both government and management. The thesis that government is potentially an effective instrument of collective problem solving, which plays a role in Schick's critique of the pattern of attention allocation at high levels of government and administration, is embedded within the public philosophy of governance sometimes referred to as Progressive Public Administration (PPA). A contemporary statement of this public philosophy is contained in Moore's *Creating Public Value: Strategic Management in Government* (1995).

Schick draws ideas from two major schools of thought on management: strategic management and management accounting and control. These schools of thought are neither scientific theories in the usual sense nor simply professional wisdom. They are well-developed traditions of argumentation about how complex organizations should be managed. Each school of thought is expressed in a substantial professional literature, much of it written by academics. Indeed, it could be argued that each school of thought is a discipline within the field of management.

Incorporating Managerial Schools of Thought

Strategic management is centered on the executive function as a whole. This function includes the formation of strategies for organizations at the business and corporate levels. In the private sector context, a strategy is often conceived as a plan for achieving sustainable competitive advantage. In government, a strategy is sometimes conceived as a pattern of decisions geared to creating public value. Some strands of strategic management thought argue that strategies should be consciously formulated and visibly endorsed by top decision makers. This approach also accepts the presumption that the effect of any given policy choice depends on other choices; in other words, policies are potentially complements. The executive function, to be well performed, requires that a wide array of choices—for example, overall objectives, measures of merit for business processes, management control systems, and improvement plans—should be aligned.

Management accounting and control encompasses a large proportion of the executive function—all but the making of fundamental strategic decisions, on the one hand, and production management, in the narrowest sense of the term, on the other (Anthony 1965). Core interests of management accounting and control include the systematic generation of nonfinancial accounting information, to be used internally for purposes of attention directing, decision making, and score keeping (Simon 1954). A closely related interest is in the design and operation of management control systems, especially in the context of complex, decentralized organizations. Such control systems include budgeting, cost accounting, reporting, and performance appraisal processes. Both scientific and practical developments have produced significant change in the field of management accounting and control over recent decades (Emmanuel and Otley 1996; Kaplan and Cooper 1998).

Learning from Experience

From Schick's theoretical standpoint, the first wave of reforms in New Zealand earned a clean—if qualified—bill of health. Changes in public management policies provided a basis for improved performance planning, including requirements that ministers and chief executives of government departments together formulate annual performance objectives for chief executives. The revamped budgetary process also provided several tools to support improved performance planning. These tools included describing organizational activity in terms of "outputs" and adopting accrual accounting methods so that budgetary charges would reflect the rate of consumption of fixed assets. With these practices, budgets authorized the consumption of a given value of resources to produce a certain type of output within a specified time frame, and in this sense, budgets constituted performance plans.

Although these measures provided a platform for performance planning on a large scale, Schick identified two main limitations to the technique. First, performance plans encoded in budgets were typically formulated without the benefit of cost accounting information, which concerns the value of resources consumed in performing activities and/or producing outputs. Output budgeting and cost analysis, in other words, are not equivalent practices. Schick argued that output budgets are somewhat arbitrary performance plans, since they are not necessarily informed by systematic measurement and analysis of the cost of government's business processes. This argument was rooted in the discipline of management accounting and control. Second, by focusing on outputs, ministers and top officials paid insufficient attention to outcomes—that is, planning for policy accomplishments. This concern was primarily rooted in the PPA thesis that government is potentially an instrument of collective betterment, reinforced by the strategic management thesis that all organizational activity is ideally geared to achieving strategic, corporate goals. Schick went on to argue that the unbalanced attention to outputs was being partially redressed by the launching of a government-wide strategic planning process in the early 1990s.

TAKING NPM FORWARD

Schick's study of New Zealand demonstrates that rigorous arguments about public management policies can be made on the basis of what economists often refer to as the traditional management literature. In this way, Schick casts doubt on the claim that the New Institutional Economics (NIE) should be regarded as the intellectual foundation of New Public Management (see point 4, above). However, the question remains whether rigorous argumentation about public management policy can take place on a large scale without the benefit of a "paradigm" such as the NIE.

From Paradigmatic Coherence to Interdisciplinary Dialogue

The crucial property of the economic approach is that it provides a basis for a coherent discussion of the full range of management controls in government, including organizational structure. The unifying force of the economic approach is attributable to the paradigmatic coherence of economics, generally, and to the specific practice of modeling organizations as collections of individuals whose choices are determined by the incentives they face. This conceptual framework ignores fields of discourse that grew up around specific administrative functions, such as budgeting, personnel management, and evaluation. After all, management controls generate incentives irrespective of the specific administrative function to which they primarily relate. This framework helped formulate the policy question of how to optimize the whole system of incentives and controls operating in government—a different question from how to improve budgeting, personnel management, and evaluation as isolated elements. The same framework provided a basis for answering this policy question as well.

The vitality of NPM as a field of policy research depends crucially on broadening its intellectual foundations beyond economic theories of organization while safeguarding the advantages of the economics approach. As a practical matter, this challenge falls to specialists in public management based in the distinct fields of public administration, management, and accounting. However, they face the inherent problems of conducting an interdisciplinary policy dialogue. Such difficulties have been redressed to some extent in other policy fields where policy knowledge is drawn from several different academic disciplines and professional communities; they should not be insuperable in the public management policy field, as I suggested in chapters 4 and 5. If the challenge of interdisciplinary dialogue is not met, the economics approach to public management policy is likely to predominate.

The method used in chapters 4 and 5 to discuss arguments on NPM is a potentially valuable tool. In some ways, the method is elementary. One requirement is to be clear about the subject, nature, and scope of claims (see chapter 4). Do the claims relate to public management policy or to the exercise of executive leadership in government? Are the claims theoretical, or are they particular evaluations? Are theoretical claims meant to apply to all types of governmental systems, or just some? Another guideline is borrowed from economics (as well as political theory): for purposes of effective communication, outline the structure of the arguments in a general way before specifying the details. A third guideline is to debug arguments that would otherwise founder on unacknowledged paradigm conflicts; this guideline applies forcefully to ambitious arguments that draw together multiple fields of discourse, as demonstrated in chapters 4 and 5. By following these guidelines, it may be possible for the NPM field of discourse to (NPM_2, NPM_3) draw on a suitably wide range of ideas about government and management while sustaining the sort of coherent discussion of public management policy that was achieved in practice in New Zealand (NPM_1).

Beyond the Anglo-American Model

This method for discussion has the additional advantage of addressing the complaint, mentioned earlier, that NPM is the

Anglo-American model of public management. If NPM is defined as a field of discussion, its essence lies in a commitment to serious argumentation, not to particular substantive foundations or conclusions. The broad structure of a serious argument might be expressed as follows:

(1) $P_i = A\,(E_i, F_i)$
(2) $E_i = A\,(S_i, T_i)$
(3) $T_i = A\,(\bullet)$, where
P_i means policy proposals for a given country i
E_i means the evaluation of current policy in country i
F_i means the feasibility of policy change in country i
S_i means a survey of current policy in country i
T_i means the theoretical basis for assessing policy in country i
$(\bullet)$ means the bodies of thought on which T_i draws

The complaint that NPM is an Anglo-American model might be interpreted as an assumption that $(\bullet)$ in expression (3) must be specified in a particular way—for example, in terms of a particular public philosophy of governance. However, an abstract conception of NPM means that a policy analyst simply needs to be clear about the basis for T_i.

The unit of argument represented by expression (3) resembles the broad approach taken in chapter 5 if $(\bullet)$ is specified as follows:

(3′) $T_i = A\,(PPG, MAN, K_G)$, where
PPG means a public philosophy of governance
MAN means schools of thought about management
K_G means empirical knowledge about governmental processes, including policy implementation

All three terms can be specified or "customized" to fit the analyst's view about the context in which public management policies are to be evaluated and devised. The term *knowledge of government* (K_G), for instance, allows account to be taken of specificities in the structure of the governmental system under analysis. Differences in governmental systems are pronounced, even within the so-called Anglo-American context (as between the Westminster-type parliamentary and the U.S. separation-of-powers systems). The term *PPG* allows consideration of national traditions of thought about government. For example, public philosophies of governance may differ substantially between institutional states, sovereign states, and corporate-bargaining states (March and Olsen 1989). Differences in the specification of *MAN*, on the other hand, may be relatively modest, although it is well known that the specific content of management thought varies among national settings (Guillén 1994). Therefore, the objection that NPM is an Anglo-American model can be laid to rest provided that NPM is conceptualized abstractly as a field of discussion about policy interventions within government and provided that high standards of argumentation are routinely practiced.

From Isolated Case Studies to Comparative Research

A critical factor for enriching policy debates about NPM is to develop and assimilate high-grade knowledge about the policymaking dynamics that drive the public management policy innovation. This knowledge can be developed through the comparative study of public management policy change. The immediate task of such studies is to explain similarities and differences among cases. A logical way forward is for individual studies to compare one or more cases with the NPM Benchmark Case—the composite of the United Kingdom, Australia, and New Zealand cases developed in chapter 3. The specific results of research along these lines are limited historical generalizations, arrived at through comparative research methods. The field of NPM will then possess an understanding of the causal effects of such factors as policy images (such as systemic organizational inefficiency), policy spillover and interference effects, policy subsystems, and policy entrepreneurship. Such an understanding can enlighten analysis of the feasibility of policy change in particular settings.

The major obstacle to policy research along these lines is perhaps the relative lack of interest in the subject of public management policy displayed by political scientists (for notable exceptions, see Campbell and Halligan 1992; Schwartz 1994a, 1994b; Zifcak 1994; Hood 1996; and Kettl 1998). For their part, public administrationists have not dedicated themselves to explaining policy change in as systematic a manner as is required of a practicing political scientist in the field of comparative politics/public policy. I hope that both political scientists and public administrationists will be drawn to this line of research.

In sum, the fundamental limitation of scholarship on the New Public Management is that it has yet to become a vital area of policy research. This book has sought to demonstrate that making a decisive turn toward a policy approach is desirable *and* feasible, at least in the area of public management policy. To adopt the policy approach is a way for scholars to contribute to the policy-making process while also strengthening the intellectual tradition that Aaron Wildavsky did so much to shape.

NOTES

CHAPTER ONE

1. All the works included in the literature review of chapter 2 fall substantially within this category; the analysis presented in chapter 3 fits squarely within it.

2. This approach is less institutionally oriented than are comparative studies whose aim is to explain persistent policy differences among cases. "Cross-national studies in new institutionalism tend toward the study of comparative statics; that is, they explain different policy outcomes in different countries with reference to their respective (stable) institutional configurations. . . . The critical inadequacy of institutional analysis to date has been a tendency toward mechanical, static accounts that largely bracket the issue of change and sometimes lapse inadvertently into institutional determinism" (Steinmo, Thelen, and Longstreth 1992, 14–16).

3. This statement does not apply specifically to Aucoin's and Hood's subsequent work on NPM, but only to the cited articles. Unfortunately, the latter work (e.g., Aucoin 1995; Hood 1996) is not nearly as well known as the seminal articles.

4. *Limited historical generalizations* is the term used by Ragin (1987) to describe what is learned from case-oriented research in political and social science.

5. Alex Matheson, Head of Division, Budgeting and Management, Public Management Service (PUMA), Organization for Economic Cooperation and Development (OECD), personal communication.

6. Formalization of explanatory arguments is a hallmark of the economics profession. The quasi-formalization of nonexplanatory policy arguments is, similarly, a communication device, borrowed to indicate how practical inferences are drawn from warrants or presumptions (Majone 1989; Walton 1992; Dunn 1994).

CHAPTER TWO

1. The new Department of Employment, Education, and Training is taken to be an institutional embodiment of the claim that relations among policy domains should be hierarchically arranged—with education nested within labor market policy, and labor market policy, in turn, nested within macroeconomic policy. The elimination of the statutory education boards—on which the education profession had been well represented—underscored the point.

2. Finance was not organizationally subordinated to Treasury, which was responsible for economic policy. The Department of Finance defined itself not only as guardian of the public purse but also as the machinery for translating economic policy into public expenditure decisions. The two organizations worked closely together, as did their ministers, both of whom were members of the economic rationalist faction of the Labor Party.

3. The book also includes a case study on the corresponding policy events in the United Kingdom.

4. Campbell and Wilson state that "the strongest symbiosis between the government and mandarinate took place in the Treasury" (1995, 40).

5. This is also a point made by Savoie (1994) in his discussion of public sector management reform in Canada.

6. Aucoin cites Roberts (1996) on the problems this policy encountered in implementation.

7. One wonders whether the government's use of public personnel policy as a way to engage in cleavage management is an additional reason.

8. Tensions between factions within the government eventually led to Holmberg's departure in 1990.

9. This statement does not specifically consider reform in the Länder in the former German Democratic Republic.

10. The tenor of the policy dialogue even influences those writers, such as Olsen (1996), who challenge the presumption that systemic organizational change in executive government is desirable.

11. Some might assume that policy choices can be described by the familiar themes of New Public Management, such as letting managers manage, managing for results, injecting competition, and so on (Schwartz 1994a, 1994b), but I would argue that themes and policy choices are analytically distinct (Barzelay and Hassel 1994). Themes come into play in the rationalization of a set of policy choices as a complementary bundle (Hirschman 1963), while policy choices are intended to alter organizational routines (Levitt and March 1990).

CHAPTER THREE

1. As indicated in the previous chapter, changes in public management policies in each of those countries differ in their specifics. For example, the United Kingdom and New Zealand split policy and operational activities through the reorganizing of government departments and the machinery of government, respectively, while Australia integrated programmatically related departments, for example, creating a two-tier ministry of employment and education. No attempt will be made to explain differences in the specific policy choices made in these countries.

2. *Limited historical generalizations* is Ragin's (1987) shorthand expression for what he elsewhere calls "modest empirical generalizations about historically-defined categories of social phenomena" (31).

3. Historical institutionalism is distinct from rational choice institutionalism and the new institutionalism in sociology (see Hall and Taylor 1996) and is closely associated with advances in the study of comparative politics and public policy (Weaver and Rockman 1993; Silberman 1993; Rothstein 1996; Nelson 1996).

4. In case-oriented research, defining case outcomes is analogous to identifying dependent variables: just as variable-oriented research is intended to explain dependent variables, work in case-oriented research is intended to explain case outcomes (Ragin 1987). Unlike variables in an economic or social theory, case outcomes in case-oriented research are historically defined phenomena, like a revolution (Skocpol 1979).

5. The term *processual model* is borrowed from Whittington (1993). Among the social scientists most closely identified with processual models of decision making are Herbert A. Simon, James G. March, and Charles E. Lindblom. The processual approach has recently been outlined in March and Olsen (1989). An important specification is Cyert and March's (1963) organizational process model, which portrays decisions as equilibria in an ongoing process of mutual adjustment among actors in organizational roles. This specification is incorporated into Allison's (1971) classic analysis of the Cuban Missile Crisis as Model II; it is also incorporated into my model of the politicized market economy (Barzelay 1986). How processual models relate to organization theory is discussed in Perrow (1986); how they relate to theories of policymaking is discussed in Lane (1990).

6. Codification, discussed theoretically by Boisot (1998), is a reason to incorporate Kingdon's model into the explanatory framework developed here, as few prospective contributors to the present research effort will have apprenticed as scholars working within historical institutionalism.

7. As these examples indicate, belief formation is a key "social mechanism" (Hedström and Swedberg 1998, 28) linking policy entrepreneurs' actions to policy change.

8. For Kingdon's extensive discussion of policy entrepreneurship, see pp. 179–182 of his text. The idea that policy entrepreneurship is a function deserves more emphasis than he conveys, but is discussed by Roberts and King (1996, 10–11).

9. A related theoretical issue—agency versus structure—figures prominently in recent methodological debates within historical institutionalism (Hay and Wincott 1998; Hall and Taylor 1998).

10. The type of policy subsystem most discussed by Baumgartner and Jones is the policy monopoly. This theoretically defined situation is illustrated with the empirical case of atomic energy policy in the 1950s and 1960s. In this case, the policy subsystem was dominated by two institutional venues, namely the Atomic Energy Commission and Congress's Joint Committee on Atomic Energy. The commonalities and differences between a "policy monopoly" and related concepts in the American political science literature are discussed in their book (7–9).

11. The breadth of a domain relates to beliefs about issue interrelatedness. See Baumgartner and Jones's discussion of the emergence of "cities" as a national policy issue.

12. Baumgartner and Jones argue that their analysis integrates the study of policy subsystems with Kingdon's model of the policy-making process: "Kingdon provides a 'close-up' view of the infusion of new ideas into the policy process and is convincing in his arguments that problems and solutions ought to be analyzed separately in order to understand governmental decision-making. At the systems level, however, agenda-setting is part of the same process of policymaking that produces stability in other cases. New policies are not continually adopted because many are simply variants on a theme that has been pursued in the past. When a general principle of policy action is in place, policymaking tends to assume an incremental character. When new principles

are under consideration, the policy-making process tends to be volatile, and Kingdon's model is most relevant" (5).

13. For a cogent empirical argument supporting this point, see Weir (1992).

14. Issue images have pervasive consequences for government's response to policy problems (see Nelson 1984; Loseke 1992; and Mashaw and Harfst 1990).

15. The idea of multicase narratives is discussed by Abbott (1992, 72–80). In his terms, each of the cases discussed here is a narrative. The Benchmark Case refers to a "common narrative appearing across the cases" (73). This argument relies on accepting the research design, including *(a)* the delineation of cases of "public management policy-making" within their respective environments and *(b)* the explanatory framework in terms of which the case narratives are crafted and compared.

16. For a parallel description, see Barzelay (1992), chapter 2. The concept of burden of proof in argumentation theory is discussed in detail in Gaskins (1992).

17. It should be pointed out that the concept of policy subsystem normally refers to a situation where central decision makers do not participate in policy-making. However, if the concept of policy subsystem is treated as a radial category (Rosch 1977; Collier and Mahon 1993), it can be stretched to include this case.

18. As Campbell and Wilson (1995) argue, Thatcher was keen not only to identify policy solutions, but also to develop an unconventional style of prime ministerial leadership in the U.K. context. The analytical focus in this chapter, however, is on public management policy-making, not executive leadership.

19. A further push of this explanation would have to account for Thatcher's beliefs as well as her opportunities (Elster 1998). (In Kingdon's model, the beliefs of policy entrepreneurs are exogenously determined.) For a discussion of Thatcher's beliefs, see Metcalfe (1993). The major factors accounting for opportunities, in this case, were the out-

come of the 1979 general election and Thatcher's prerogatives as the leader of the majority party and prime minister.

20. *Co-opetition* is a neologism that refers to a mixture of cooperation and competition (Nalebuff and Brandenburger 1997).

21. Australia's program went further than the U.K.'s program did; it included changes in the running cost system along with the mandated "efficiency dividend," as discussed in chapter 2.

22. This interpretation draws primarily on Campbell and Halligan (1992).

23. The shaping of the problem definition involved policy entrepreneurship in both cases. In Australia, this function was apparently performed by a larger number of actors than in the U.K. case.

24. In his coauthored books, Colin Campbell identifies several relevant factors: the earlier hiving off of Australia's Finance Department from Treasury; the professional composition and ethos of the Finance Department, which was vastly different from the U.K. Treasury; and the vitality with which departmental leaders—ministers and officials—sought to perform the functions of executive leadership.

25. For a discussion of differences in these related arguments, see Breton (1996).

26. By this interpretation, Australia and New Zealand arrived at similar problem definitions by different routes, namely a spillover from fiscal policy in the former and conviction in the latter.

27. Institutional comparisons among the United Kingdom, Australia, and New Zealand are discussed in Campbell and Wilson (1995) as well as in Campbell (1997).

28. A similar, complementary argument is that the Next Steps Initiative resulted from political learning (Hood 1996). Hood argues that the Conservatives under Thatcher learned that privatizing public enterprises was politically attractive and feasible. Experience with privatization emboldened the government to reorganize the core public sector. In Kingdon's terms, Next Steps was a spillover from privatization.

29. On this point, see Campbell and Wilson (1995) and Aucoin (1995).

30. This mismatch might have been resolved by reducing aspirations (Hirschman 1963; Elster 1983). The downward stickiness of aspirations is attributable to the stability of the political and problem streams and, in turn, to policy entrepreneurship.

31. The evaluative question of whether this situation was desirable is discussed in Campbell and Wilson (1995). See also chapter 2 of this text.

32. If we accept Pusey's (1991) account, this same statement applies equally to the Australia case. On the other hand, Campbell and Halligan's (1992) account suggests that the belief that the core public sector was inefficient was the result of the government's overall political and policy strategy rather than a "conviction" in the ordinary sense.

33. Domain unification invited systemic analysis of the problem of public service inefficiency. Candidate ideas to address this problem naturally touched on a wide range of managerial and administrative systems, including microbudgeting and financial control systems, accounting information systems, organizational structure, employment arrangements, procurement policies, compensation policies, goal-setting activities, and the audit function. A fuller discussion of domain unification would point out that managerial and economics ideas, which were influential in these cases, transcended conventional categories of expenditure planning and financial management, civil service and labor relations, procurement, organization and methods, and audit and evaluation.

34. Sweden did not reorganize the machinery of government. These arrangements, which included an organizational demarcation between policy ministries and agencies, were deeply embedded in constitutional practice.

35. A significant prior contribution to the policy stream was Kelman's (1990) *Procurement and Public Management.* In 1993, Kelman was appointed to head the Office of Federal Procurement Policy. For details on policy ideas in this area, see Kelman (1994).

36. The concept of partial equilibrium also applies to changes in department- or agency-specific institutional rules and routines related to public management—acquisition reform in the Defense Department, for instance. However, such episodes of policy-making are defined in this study as outside the scope of public management policy, falling instead within the scope of so-called substantive policy areas, such as defense, environment, education, and the like.

37. This subsection is based on discussions with Natascha Fuechtner, a doctoral student at the Speyer graduate school of public administration in Germany, and Florian Lennert, a doctoral student at the London School of Economics.

38. The repercussions of this historic event proved substantial at the local level in the Länder of the former West Germany, since municipalities bore the brunt of spending reductions. The diffusion of the New Steering Model, discussed in the previous chapter, owes much to this downstream effect.

39. For background on these principles of German federal administration, see Katzenstein (1987).

40. Sweden may be an interesting point of comparison for Germany, as these properties seem to characterize both cases. On the other hand, Sweden developed a unified public management policy domain. Why? Because of initial conditions, with Sweden's Ministry of Finance enjoying a wider range of prerogatives than its German counterpart? Because the Swedish government in the late 1980s was under the control of a single party rather than a coalition? Because Sweden experienced impulses in the Political Stream (A1) sufficient to bring about a disequilibrium situation? Or because public management policy-making in Sweden proceeded without the interference of unification policies? These explanations are not mutually exclusive; indeed they are linked. My inclination is to stress the absence of a disequilibrium situation in Germany and, hence, factors in the Political Stream (A1) and the role of agenda congestion, spillover, and interference effects.

41. The research goal, which is to understand public management policy change, can usefully be pursued through various research designs, such as a single case study emphasizing the role and process of executive leadership (e.g., Campbell and Halligan 1992). My approach is specifically designed to yield generalizations based on the systematic comparative analysis of cases.

42. A study analyzing change in economic policy on a comparative basis is Katzenstein (1978); it was an important contribution to the international political economy literature and greatly influenced my own single case study of changes in Brazil's energy policies (Barzelay 1986). The conclusions of my study qualified the generalizations developed by Katzenstein on the basis of analysis of an additional case. The function that Katzenstein's study performed in the economic policy literature has not been fulfilled by recent comparative studies of management reform in government, including March and Olsen (1989), Pollitt (1993), Savoie (1994), and Olsen and Peters (1996). The absence of a work like Katzenstein's is a factor limiting the value of single case studies on public management policy. The present chapter is designed to fill the gap.

CHAPTER FOUR

1. Page numbers introduced in the text of this chapter refer to Aucoin's (1995) book *The New Public Management: Canada in Comparative Perspective*.

2. This quote is drawn from a section that begins with a discussion of "ideological and intellectual attacks on the policy foundations of the modern state." Later, in his chapter 4, agency theory is discussed as follows: "Agency theory is appealing because it provides the theoretical justification for delegated authority to government departments in order to promote productivity in the use of resources in pursuit of organizational missions. . . . Agency theory is appealing because it emphasizes transparency in ministerial–public service relations: ministers decide

what they want to see accomplished and then contract with their public service managers to deliver the results" (107). Aucoin thus conveys the impression that he regards agency theory as providing backing for the claims he makes about governance and public management.

3. Since Aucoin's chapters mix descriptions of public management policies with the context surrounding policy change in Australia, New Zealand, the United Kingdom, and Canada; with policy commentary; and with normative public administration theory, a clear line of argumentation can be discerned only with interpretation. I believe I have been true to his intentions, yet caveats apply—the most important of which is that I assume "agency theory" refers to the economic theory of agency as explicated, for example, in Breton (1996, 155–162).

4. See Aucoin's reference 19 on page 46.

5. Literal principal-agent contracts and legal codes regulating principal-agent relations typically specify impermissible and required actions as well. The economic theory of agency is exclusively concerned with permissible actions, which makes sense given that the defining assumption is that actions are unobserved. On this point, as well as others, I benefited from discussions with James Montgomery.

6. As can be seen, *output* gets its meaning from the theoretical discussion of principal-agent relations rather than from such other frames of reference as production management.

7. These points are stated so as to highlight what might be taken to be the connection between the economic theory of agency and Aucoin's claims.

8. Lindblom (1990, 24) captures this distinction by distinguishing standing volitions from action volitions. In this context, standing volitions refer to statements about types of situations and indefinite temporal horizons, while action volitions refer to statements about particular situations and, naturally, to specific times and places.

9. Aucoin's specification of managerialism differs considerably from that of Pollitt (1993), who uses managerialism mainly to refer to

scientific management. This difference can be attributed, in part, to the fact that Pollitt was writing in a U.K. context while Aucoin was writing in a North American one.

10. Saying that PPA is an element of *A* (•) might appear to fly in the face of Hood's (1994) contention that PPA became "extinct" in the 1980s. However, Aucoin's project is different from Hood's in that it defends an administrative argument rather than describes or explains a policy process or outcome. The contention that PPA became extinct or that its ideas were repudiated in the 1980s has no bearing on whether PPA should be considered in fashioning a theory of public management policy. On this point, see also Peters and Wright (1996).

11. Aucoin does not identify transaction cost economics as a strand of NIE, for reasons that may have to do with the scope of his argument: he is centrally concerned with public management policies for the whole of government. He is not much concerned with program design decisions taken at the departmental level.

12. In the concluding section of the same chapter, Aucoin adds: "When public servants exercise great power in the design and implementation of public policy, it is invariably as a consequence of the political leadership devolving authority to them and usually because a consensus exists between ministers and public servants as to the general direction of public policy" (45).

13. I have called attention to assumptions about the decision, rather than information, structure of principal-agent models because Aucoin's conclusions about what ministers should do as overseers of government departments do not depend on any assumptions about the information structure. A decision structure of delegation is sufficient to support his argument.

14. The specific nature of the agency problem depends on details of the particular principal-agent model.

15. In economic theory, actors in a situation are depicted as individuals rather than as people whose social relations are defined by their roles (Montgomery 1998).

16. Culture theory is the basis of Hood's (1998) recent theoretical discussion of public management generally and NPM in particular.

17. Hood (1998) describes PPA as a hierarchist approach to public management.

18. This term is selected because the "survey of practice" is a venerable tradition of scholarship in public administration, as illustrated by Willoughby (1918), White (1933), and Schick (1990).

19. The standard relates to the unresolved question about whether bureaus and firms should be assimilated into the broader category of *organizations* and, similarly, about the extent to which government and industries should be assimilated into the larger category of the *economy*. The standard also relates to the plausibility of claims that are backed by warrants of best or smart practice *within* the public sector (Bardach 1998).

20. Similarly, the structure of the argument represented by expression (6) might be described as follows: *P* refers to public management policies that the Canadian federal government should adopt and implement, where *P* includes all favorably evaluated policies (*E*) not observed in the survey of public management policies in Canada (*S*).

21. Readers who want to take semantics seriously may wish to consult Lakoff (1987), Lakoff (1996), and Lakoff and Johnson (1999).

CHAPTER FIVE

1. Wilson's "theory" of bureaucracy is a synthesis of case-oriented empirical research rather than a body of propositions derived from axiomatic assumptions. The primary conceptual scheme is a system of interacting political institutions, organizations, and occupational roles. Political institutions include Congress, organizations are bureaus and departments, and occupational roles include operators, managers, and executives.

2. Although contingency theory is controversial in organizational studies, it has tended to benefit management theory and doctrine. For

interesting arguments based on contingency theory, see Mintzberg (1983) and Macintosh (1994).

3. Although Wilson's typology echoes agency theory, his conceptual framework is substantially different. His distinction between *output* and *outcome* is not the same as the distinction between *effort* and *output* in agency theory. Whereas "output" for Wilson is a performed task, "output" in agency theory is that which principals and agents decide to measure for purposes of determining rewards. "Output" in Wilson gets its meaning from a work scenario, while "output" in agency theory draws its meaning from a bargaining scenario. Wilson's conceptual framework echoes scientific management and the Carnegie School of organization theory; principal-agent theory is New Institutional Economics. Wilson's text does not prepare the reader for such conceptual differences.

4. In Wilson's case, delegation is from overseers to bureaus, whereas in Aucoin's case delegation is from ministers to the public service, reflecting differences between the governmental systems about which they are writing.

5. For a discussion of the temporal structure of policy implementation, see Moore (1995), chapter 2.

6. Aucoin says that the public service knows more about how to implement public policy than do ministers, but that point is radically different from the notion that programmatic effects often take time to occur.

7. Schick admittedly discusses NIE, but only to describe and explain the New Zealand reforms.

8. For textbook discussions of management accounting and control, see Hongren, Sundem, and Stratton (1996) and Macintosh (1994). For a discussion of strategic management and business policy, see Whittington (1993); Rumelt, Schendel, and Teece (1994); Mintzberg (1994); and Mintzberg, Ahlstrand, and Lampel (1998). For a stimulating effort to interrelate MAC and SM, see Simons (1995).

9. Schick writes: "According to the logic of New Zealand reform [*sic*], government should negotiate a price for outputs, as is done in market exchanges, and pay on the basis of the volume of goods and services to be supplied. This logic has led it to mirror the market by budgeting and appropriating for outputs.... 'Pricing' operations in terms of input costs has been discredited, but the new system of 'pricing outputs' remains underdeveloped.... The government has assumed that departments were so inefficient in the past that they can now operate with lower staffing levels and without compensation for inflation.... 'Doing more for less' in real terms would be more reasonably justified if the government had adequate cost accounting systems to analyze the cost of producing outputs. In most government departments, however, managers do not know what the unit cost of outputs is or should be" (63–65).

10. Schick writes: "The SRAs have assisted the government to deal with one of the most difficult requirements of the reforms—the specification of outcomes. Although many of the SRAs are too broadly drawn to qualify as outcome statements, substantial progress has been made" (61).

11. As a reminder, Aucoin's theory of public management policy is structured by PPA, agency theory, and WPO. Schick's is structured by PPA, MAC, and SM.

12. Aucoin includes a related discussion (159–60). However, its connection to his argument about public management policy is tenuous.

13. Schick writes: "Ministers and managers must agree in advance on financial performance and outputs to be produced, the money to be spent on the agreed outputs, and the quality and timeliness of the work to be performed. This advance specification of performance enables Ministers and managers to compare the volume, cost, and quality of the outputs actually produced to planned levels. This is the essence of managerial accountability—doing what was contracted at the agreed price and explaining any variance between planned and actual performance.... Much effort has been expended by departments in developing detailed output

information.... Without trend or comparative data, [however,] it is hard to interpret or analyze the output information. If all that is wanted is specification of outputs, so that actual performance can be compared to targets, the present arrangement is satisfactory" (74–77). Schick goes on to argue that the emphasis could usefully shift from compliance to improvement.

14. Schick writes: "The two approaches [i.e., contractualist and managerialist] go their separate ways... in the emphasis placed on employment contracts, purchase and performance agreements, in the decoupling of policy advice from service delivery, the emphasis on ex ante specification, the sharp split between purchase and ownership and between outputs and outcomes, and the demanding accountability requirements. Managerial concepts explain most of the innovations introduced in New Zealand, but not the most conspicuous ones. Arguably, the reforms inspired by a managerial perspective have brought most of the State sector improvement over the past decade" (23).

15. Because of the present volume's focus on public management policies, the line of argument about the "organizational intervention" in Minnesota's staff agencies merits only a brief discussion. If *BTB* had been written a few years later, it would have been possible to refer to general arguments on the subject of executive leadership in government and the specific topic of managing change in government from a position of executive authority (Moore 1995; Roberts and King 1996). From this standpoint, the intervention in Minnesota was praiseworthy for winning acceptance of changes in institutional rules and routines from the employees of central staff organizations, from attentive legislative overseers, and from executives across the government. Some features of the specific intervention in Minnesota are especially notable, including the presentation to legislative overseers of an overall strategy for managing Department of Administration activities and the document explaining the problem-solving approach to staffing, both of which were included as appendices to that book.

16. These observations are based on comments by Nathalie Halgand.

CHAPTER SIX

1. The characterization of NPM presented here is more abstract than conventional academic accounts are. I have not defined NPM in terms of specific policy principles, such as separating policy-making from operational activities, nor as a response to any historically specific challenge to governmental systems, such as fiscal stress and the globalization of the international economy. Nor have I defined NPM as a paradigm for reforming institutional aspects of government, or in terms of typical policy interventions such as financial management improvement programs, bureaucratic reorganizations, and changing the focus of central audit activities. At the same time, the definition of NPM presented here is less broad than ones that include changes in programmatic content and a reduction in the scope of public sector activities.

2. By contrast, the U.K. case was viewed as one where the government imitated a business model of management.

3. Walter Kickert of Erasmus University in the Netherlands is well known for expressing this point of view.

4. The concept of standpoint in this context is equivalent to "theory of public management policy" as this term is used in chapters 4 and 5.

REFERENCES

Abbott, Andrew. 1992. "What Do Cases Do? Some Notes on Activity in Sociological Analysis." In *What Is a Case? Exploring the Foundations of Social Inquiry*, ed. Charles C. Ragin and Howard S. Becker. Cambridge: Cambridge University Press.

Allison, Graham T., Jr. 1971. *Essence of Decision*. Boston: Little, Brown.

Anthony, Robert N. 1965. *Planning and Control Systems: A Framework for Analysis*. Boston: Division of Research, Gradute School of Business Administration, Harvard University.

Aucoin, Peter. 1990. "Administrative Reform in Public Management: Paradigms, Principles, Paradoxes, and Pendulums." *Governance* 3 (2): 115–137.

———. 1995. *The New Public Management: Canada in Comparative Perspective*. Montreal: IRPP.

Bardach, Eugene. 1998. *Getting Agencies to Work Together: The Practice and Theory of Managerial Craftsmanship*. Washington, DC: Brookings.

Barzelay, Michael. 1986. *The Politicized Market Economy: Alcohol in Brazil's Energy Strategy*. Berkeley: University of California Press.

———. 1992. *Breaking Through Bureaucracy: A New Vision for Managing in Government*. Berkeley: University of California Press.

Barzelay, Michael, and Bryan Hassel. 1994. "Revamping Public Management: Improving Comparative Research." Paper presented at Tenth Anniversary Conference of the Structure and Organization of Government Section of the International Political Science Association, Manchester University.

Barzelay, Michael, and George Lakoff. 1995. "Should Customer Satisfaction Be a Goal of Public Organizations?" Paper presented at the Annual Research Conference of the Association of Public Policy Analysis and Management (APPAM), Chicago, IL.

Baumgartner, Frank R., and Bryan D. Jones. 1993. *Agendas and Instability in American Politics.* Chicago: University of Chicago Press.

Benz, Arthur, and Klaus H. Goetz. 1996. "The German Public Sector: National Priorities and the International Reform Agenda." In *A New German Public Sector? Reform, Adaptation, and Stability*, ed. Arthur Benz and Klaus H. Goetz. Aldershot, England: Dartmouth.

Boisot, Max. 1998. *Knowledge Assets.* Oxford: Oxford University Press.

Boston, Jonathan. 1991. "The Theoretical Underpinnings of Public Sector Restructuring in New Zealand." In *Reshaping the State: New Zealand's Bureaucratic Revolution*, ed. Jonathan Boston, John Martin, June Pallot, and Pat Walsh. Auckland, New Zealand: Oxford University Press.

———. 1996. "Origins and Destinations: New Zealand's Model of Public Management and the International Transfer of Ideas." In *New Ideas, Better Government*, ed. Patrick Weller and Glyn Davis. Sydney: Allen and Unwin.

Boston, Jonathan, John Martin, June Pallot, and Pat Walsh. 1991. *Reshaping the State: New Zealand's Bureaucratic Revolution.* Auckland, New Zealand: Oxford University Press.

———. 1996. *Public Management: The New Zealand Model.* Auckland, New Zealand: Oxford University Press.

Breton, Albert. 1996. *Competitive Governments: An Economic Theory of Politics and Public Finance.* Cambridge: Cambridge University Press.

Campbell, Colin. 1997. "Bringing Strategic Decision Making into Planning and Budgeting." Washington, DC: World Bank Public Management Unit.

Campbell, Colin, and John Halligan. 1992. *Political Leadership in an Age of Constraint: The Australian Experience.* Pittsburgh, PA: University of Pittsburgh Press.

Campbell, Colin, and Graham K. Wilson. 1995. *The End of Whitehall: Death of a Paradigm?* Oxford: Blackwell.

Clarke, John, and Janet Newman. 1997. *The Managerial State: Power, Politics, and Ideology in the Remaking of Social Welfare.* London: Sage.

Cohen, Michael, James March, and J. P. Olsen. 1972. "A Garbage Can Model of Organizational Choice." *Administrative Sciences Quarterly* 17 (1): 1–25.

Collier, David, and James E. Mahon, Jr. 1993. "Conceptual 'Stretching' Revisited: Adapting Categories in Comparative Analysis." *American Political Science Review* 87 (4): 845–855.

Cyert, Richard M., and James G. March. 1963. *A Behavioral Theory of the Firm.* Englewood Cliffs, NJ: Prentice-Hall.

Derlien, Hans-Ulrich. 1996. "Patterns of Postwar Administrative Development in Germany." In *The New German Public Sector? Reform, Adaptation, and Stability,* ed. Arthur Benz and Klaus H. Goetz. Aldershot, England: Dartmouth.

Douglas, Mary. 1990. "Converging on Autonomy: Anthropology and Institutional Economics." In *Organization Theory: From Chester Barnard to the Present and Beyond,* ed. Oliver Williamson. New York: Oxford University Press.

Dunleavy, Patrick. 1991. *Democracy, Bureaucracy, and Public Choice.* Hemel Hempstead, England: Harvester Wheatsheaf.

Dunn, William N. 1994. *Public Policy Analysis,* 2d ed. Englewood Cliffs, NJ: Prentice Hall.

Elster, Jon. 1983. *Sour Grapes.* Cambridge: Cambridge University Press.

———. 1989. *Nuts and Bolts for the Social Sciences.* Cambridge: Cambridge University Press.

———. 1998. "A Plea for Mechanisms." In *Social Mechanisms: An Analytical Approach to Social Theory*, ed. Peter Hedström and Richard Swedberg. Cambridge: Cambridge University Press.

Emmanuel, Clive, and David Otley, eds. 1996. *Readings in Accounting for Management Control*, 2d ed. London: ITP.

Ferlie, Ewan, Andrew Pettigrew, Lynn Ashburner, and Louise Fitzgerald. 1996. *The New Public Management in Action.* Oxford: Oxford University Press.

Fleishman, Joel. 1990. "A New Framework for Integration: Policy Analysis and Public Management." *American Behavioral Scientist* (July-August): 733–754.

Foxley, Alejandro. 1981. "Stabilization Policies and Their Effects on Employment and Income Distribution: A Latin American Perspective." In *Economic Stabilization in Developing Countries*, ed. William R. Cline and Sidney Weintraub. Washington, DC: Brookings.

Friedman, John. 1987. *Planning in the Public Domain.* Princeton, NJ: Princeton University Press.

Gaskins, Richard H. 1992. *Burdens of Proof in Modern Discourse.* New Haven, CT: Yale University Press.

Gray, Andrew, and Bill Jenkins with Andrew Flynn and Brian Rutherford. 1991. "The Management of Change in Whitehall: The Experience of the FMI." *Public Administration* 69 (spring): 41–59.

Gregory, Robert. 1995. "Accountability, Responsibility, and Corruption: Managing the 'Public Production Process.' " In *The State under Contract*, ed. Jonathan Boston. Wellington, New Zealand: Bridget Williams Books.

Guillén, Mauro. 1994. *Models of Management.* Chicago: University of Chicago Press.

Hall, Peter A. 1992. "The Movement from Keynesianism to Monetarism: Institutional Analysis and British Economic Policy in the 1970s." In *Structuring Politics: Historical Institutionalism in Comparative Analysis*, ed. Sven Steinmo, Kathleen Thelen, and Frank Longstreth. Cambridge: Cambridge University Press.

Hall, Peter A., and Rosemary C. R. Taylor. 1996. "Political Science and the Three New Institutionalisms." *Political Studies.* 44, 4: 936–957.

———. 1998. "The Potential of Historical Institutionalism: A Response to Hay and Wincott." *Political Studies* 46: 958–962.

Hay, Colin, and Daniel Wincott. 1998. "Structure, Agency, and Historical Institutionalism." *Political Studies* 46: 951–957.

Hedström, Peter, and Richard Swedberg. 1998. "Social Mechanisms: An Introductory Essay." In *Social Mechanisms: An Analytical Approach to Social Theory*, ed. Peter Hedström and Richard Swedberg. Cambridge: Cambridge University Press.

Hirschman, Albert O. 1963. *Journeys Toward Progress.* New York: Norton.

Hongren, Charles T., Gary Sundem, and William O. Stratton. 1996. *Introduction to Management Accounting*, 10th ed. London: Prentice Hall International.

Hood, Christopher. 1986. *The Tools of Government.* Chatham, NJ: Chatham House.

———. 1991. "A Public Management for All Seasons?" *Public Administration* 69 (1): 3–19.

———. 1994. *Explaining Economic Policy Reversals.* Buckingham, England: Open University Press.

———. 1996. "United Kingdom: From Second Chance to Near-Miss Learning." In *Lessons from Experience: Experiential Learning in Administrative Reforms in Eight Democracies*, ed. Johan P. Olsen and B. Guy Peters. Oslo: Scandinavian University Press.

———. 1998. *The Art of the State: Culture, Rhetoric, and Public Management.* Oxford: Clarendon.

Hood, Christopher H., and Michael Jackson. 1991. *Administrative Argument.* Aldershot, England: Dartmouth.

———. 1994. "Keys for Locks in Administrative Argument." *Administration and Society* 25 (4): 467–488.

Horn, Murray J. 1995. *The Political Economy of Public Administration: Institutional Choice in the Public Sector.* Cambridge: Cambridge University Press.

Humphrey, Christopher, and Olov Olson. 1995. "'Caught in the Act': Public Services Disappearing in the World of 'Accountable Management.'" In *Issues in Management Accounting*, 2d ed., ed. David Ashton, Trevor Hopper, and Robert W. Scapens. Englewood Cliffs, NJ: Prentice Hall.

Immergut, Ellen M. 1992. "The Rules of the Game: The Logic of Health Policy-making in France, Switzerland, and Sweden." In *Structuring Politics: Historical Institutionalism in Comparative Analysis*, ed. Sven Steinmo, Kathleen Thelen, and Frank Longstreth. Cambridge: Cambridge University Press.

Kaplan, Robert S., and Robin Cooper. 1998. *Cost and Effect: Using Integrated Cost Systems to Drive Profitability and Performance*. Boston, MA: Harvard Business School Press.

Karl, Barry Dean. 1963. *Executive Reorganization and Reform in the New Deal: The Genesis of Administrative Management, 1900–1939*. Cambridge, MA: Harvard University Press.

Katzenstein, Peter J., ed. 1978. *Between Power and Plenty: Foreign Economic Policies of Advanced Industrial States*. Madison: University of Wisconsin Press.

Katzenstein, Peter J. 1987. *Policy and Politics in West Germany: The Growth of a Semi-Sovereign State*. Philadelphia, PA: Temple University Press.

Kelman, Steven. 1990. *Procurement and Public Management*. Washington, DC: American Enterprise Institute.

———. 1994. "Deregulating Federal Procurement: Nothing to Fear But Discretion Itself?" In *Deregulating the Public Service: Can Government Be Improved?* ed. John J. DiIulio, Jr. Washington, DC: Brookings.

Kettl, Donald F. 1995. "Building Lasting Reform: Enduring Questions, Missing Answers." In *Inside the Reinvention Machine: Appraising Governmental Reform*, ed. Donald F. Kettl and John J. DiIulio Jr. Washington, DC: Brookings.

———. 1997. "The Global Revolution in Public Management: Driving Themes, Missing Links." *Journal of Policy Analysis and Management* 16 (summer): 446–462.

———. 1998. *Reinventing Government: A Fifth-Year Report Card.* Washington, DC: Center for Public Management, Brookings Institution.

Kingdon, John. 1984. *Agendas, Alternatives, and Public Policies.* Boston: Little, Brown.

Kiser, Edgar. 1996. "The Revival of Narrative in Historical Sociology: What Rational Choice Theory Can Contribute." *Politics and Society* 24 (3): 249–271.

Klages, Helmut, and Elke Löffler. 1996. "Difficulties of Implementing the New Steering Model in German Local Government." Paper presented at the Conference on New Public Management in International Perspective, Institute of Public Finance and Fiscal Law, University of St. Gallen, Switzerland.

Knight, Frank H. 1921. *Risk, Uncertainty, and Profit.* Boston: Houghton Mifflin.

Lakoff, George. 1987. *Women, Fire, and Dangerous Things: What Categories Reveal about the Mind.* Chicago: University of Chicago Press.

———. 1996. *Moral Politics.* Chicago: University of Chicago Press.

Lakoff, George, and Mark Johnson. 1980. *Metaphors We Live By.* Chicago: University of Chicago Press.

———. 1999. *Philosophy in the Flesh.* New York: Basic Books.

Lane, Jan-Erik. 1990. *Institutional Reform: A Public Policy Perspective.* Aldershot, England: Gower.

Leonard-Barton, Dorothy. 1995. *Wellsprings of Knowledge: Building and Sustaining the Sources of Innovation.* Boston: Harvard Business School Press.

Levitt, Barbara, and James G. March. 1990. "Chester A. Barnard and the Intelligence of Learning." In *Organization Theory: From Chester Barnard to the Present and Beyond*, ed. Oliver E. Williamson. New York: Oxford University Press.

Lindblom, Charles E. 1990. *Inquiry and Change: The Troubled Attempt to Understand and Change Society.* New Haven, CT: Yale University Press.

Löffler, Elke. 1996. *The Modernization of the Public Sector in an International Comparative Perspective: Concepts and Methods of Awarding and Assessing Quality in the Public Sector in OECD Countries.* Speyer, Germany: Forschunginstitut fur Offentliche Verwaltung.

Loseke, Donileen R. 1992. *The Battered Woman and Shelters: The Social Construction of Wife Abuse.* Albany: State University of New York Press.

Lynn, Laurence E., Jr. 1996. *Public Management as Art, Science, and Profession.* Chatham, NJ: Chatham House.

Macintosh, Norman B. 1994. *Management Accounting and Control Systems: An Organizational and Behavioral Approach.* Chichester, England: Wiley.

Majone, Giandomenico. 1989. *Argument, Evidence, and Persuasion in the Policy Process.* New Haven, CT: Yale University Press.

March, James G., and Johan P. Olsen. 1989. *Rediscovering Institutions.* New York: Free Press.

Mashaw, Jerry L., and David Harfst. 1990. *The Struggle for Auto Safety.* Cambridge, MA: Harvard University Press.

McSweeney, Brendan. 1994. "Management by Accounting." In *Accounting as Social and Institutional Practice: An Introduction*, ed. Anthony Hopwood and Peter Miller. Cambridge: Cambridge University Press.

Metcalfe, Les. 1993. "Conviction Politics and Dynamic Conservatism: Mrs. Thatcher's Managerial Revolution." *International Political Science Review* 14 (4): 351–371.

Metcalfe, Les, and Sue Richards. 1987. *Improving Public Management.* London: Sage.

Meyer, John W. 1983. "On the Celebration of Rationality." *Accounting, Organizations, and Society* 8 (2/3): 235–240.

Milgrom, Paul, and John Roberts. 1992. *Economics, Organization, and Management.* Englewood Cliffs, NJ: Prentice Hall.

———. 1995. "Complementaries and Fit: Strategy, Structure, and Organizational Change in Manufacturing." *Journal of Accounting and Economics* 19: 179–208.

Mintzberg, Henry. 1983. *Designing Effective Organizations: Structures in Fives.* Englewood Cliffs, NJ: Prentice Hall.

———. 1994. *The Rise and Fall of Strategic Planning.* Englewood Cliffs, NJ: Prentice Hall.

Mintzberg, Henry, Bruce Ahlstrand, and Joseph Lampel. 1998. *Strategy Safari: A Guided Tour through the Wilds of Strategic Management.* London: Prentice Hall International.

Moctezuma Barragán, Esteban, and Andrés Roemer. 1999. *Por un Gobierno con Resultados.* Mexico City: Fondo de Cultura Económica.

Moe, Ronald. 1994. "The 'Reinventing Government' Exercise: Misinterpreting the Problem, Misjudging the Consequences." *Public Administration Review* 54 (2): 111–122.

Montgomery, James. 1998. "Toward a Role-Theoretic Conception of Embeddedness." *American Journal of Sociology* 104 (1): 92–125.

Moore, Mark H. 1995. *Creating Public Value: Strategic Management in Government.* Cambridge, MA: Harvard University Press.

Morgan, Gareth. 1983. *Images of Organizations.* London: Sage.

Nalebuff, Barry, and Adam M. Brandenburger. 1997. *Co-opetition.* New York: Doubleday.

Nelson, Barbara J. 1984. *Making an Issue of Child Abuse: Political Agenda Setting for Social Problems.* Chicago: University of Chicago Press.

———. 1996. "Public Policy and Administration: An Overview." In *The New Handbook of Political Science*, ed. Robert E. Goodin and Hans-Dieter Klingemann. Oxford: Oxford University Press.

OECD. 1996. *Performance Auditing and the Modernization of Government.* Paris: OECD.

Olsen, Johan P. 1996. "Norway: Slow Learner—or Another Triumph of the Tortoise?" In *Lessons from Experience: Experiential Learning in Administrative Reforms in Eight Democracies*, ed. Johan P. Olsen and B. Guy Peters. Oslo: Scandinavian University Press.

Olsen, Johan P., and B. Guy Peters, eds. 1996. *Lessons from Experience: Experiential Learning in Administrative Reforms in Eight Democracies.* Oslo: Scandinavian University Press.

Osborne, David, and Ted Gaebler. 1992. *Reinventing Government.* Reading, MA: Addison-Wesley.

Perrow, Charles. 1986. *Complex Organizations: A Critical Essay,* 3d ed. New York: Random House.

Peters, B. Guy, and Vincent Wright. 1996. "Public Policy and Administration, Old and New." In *A New Handbook of Political Science,* ed. Robert Goodin and Hans-Dieter Klingemann. Oxford: Oxford University Press.

Peters, Thomas, and Robert Waterman. 1982. *In Search of Excellence.* New York: Warner Books.

Pierre, Jon. 1993. "Legitimacy, Institutional Change, and the Politics of Public Administration in Sweden." *International Political Science Review* 14 (4): 387–401.

Pollitt, Christopher. 1993. *Managerialism and the Public Services: The Anglo-American Experience,* 2d ed. Oxford: Blackwell.

Power, Michael. 1997. *The Audit Society: Rituals of Verification.* Oxford: Oxford University Press.

Premfors, Rune. 1991. "The 'Swedish Model' and Public Sector Reform." *West European Politics* 14 (3): 83–95.

Przeworski, Adam. 1987. "Methods of Cross-National Research, 1970–83: An Overview." In *Comparative Policy Research: Learning from Experience,* ed. M. Dierkes, H.N. Weiler and A.B. Antal. Aldershot, England: Gower.

Pusey, Michael. 1991. *Economic Rationalism in Canberra.* New York: Cambridge University Press.

Ragin, Charles C. 1987. *The Comparative Method: Moving beyond Qualitative and Quantitative Stategies.* Berkeley: University of California Press.

Roberts, Alasdair. 1996. "Public Works and Government Services: Beautiful Theory Meets Ugly Reality." In *How Ottawa Spends,* ed. Gene Swimmer. Ottawa: Carleton University Press.

Roberts, Nancy C., and Paula J. King. 1996. *Transforming Public Policy: Dynamics of Policy Entrepreneurship and Innovation.* San Francisco: Jossey-Bass.

Robinson, Ray, and Julian LeGrand, eds. 1993. *Evaluating the NHS Reforms.* London: King's Fund Institute.

Rosch, Elinor. 1977. "Human Categorization." In *Studies in Cross-Cultural Psychology,* ed. E. Rosch and B. B. Lloyd. Hillsdale, NJ: Erlbaum.

Rothstein, Bo. 1996. "Political Institutions: An Overview." In *The New Handbook of Political Science,* ed. Robert E. Goodin and Hans-Dieter Klingemann. Oxford: Oxford University Press.

Rumelt, Richard P., Dan E. Schendel, and David J. Teece, eds. 1994. *Fundamental Issues in Strategy: A Research Agenda.* Boston: Harvard Business School Press.

Rutherford, Malcolm. 1994. *Institutions in Economics: The Old and the New Institutionalism.* Cambridge: Cambridge University Press.

Salamon, Lester, ed. 1989. *Beyond Privatization: The Tools of Government Action.* Washington, DC: Urban Institute Press.

Savoie, Donald J. 1994. *Thatcher, Reagan, Mulroney: In Search of a New Bureaucracy.* Pittsburgh, PA: University of Pittsburgh Press.

Schattschneider, E. E. 1960. *The Semi-Sovereign People.* New York: Holt, Reinhardt, and Winston.

Schick, Allen. 1990. "Budgeting for Results: Recent Developments in Five Industrialized Countries." *Public Administration Review* 50 (1): 26–34.

———. 1996. *The Spirit of Reform: Managing the New Zealand State Sector in a Time of Change.* Wellington, New Zealand: State Services Commission and the Treasury. (http://www.ssc.govt.nz)

Schumpeter, J. A. 1934. *The Theory of Economic Development.* London: Oxford University Press.

Schwartz, Herman. 1994a. "Public Choice Theory and Public Choices: Bureaucrats and State Reorganization in Australia, Denmark, New Zealand, Sweden in the 1980s." *Administration and Society* 26 (1): 48–77.

———. 1994b. "Small States in Big Trouble." *World Politics* 46 (4): 527–555.

Silberman, Bernard. 1993. *Cages of Reason: The Rise of the Rational State in France, Japan, the United States, and Great Britain.* Chicago: University of Chicago Press.

Simon, Herbert A. 1954. *Centralization versus Decentralization in Organizing the Controller's Department.* New York: Controllership Foundation.

Simons, Robert. 1995. *Levers of Control: How Managers Use Innovative Control Systems to Drive Strategic Renewal.* Boston: Harvard Business School Press.

Skocpol, Theda. 1979. *States and Social Revolutions.* Cambridge: Cambridge University Press.

Sparrow, Malcolm. 1994. *Imposing Duties.* Westport, CT: Praeger.

Steinmo, Sven, Kathleen Thelen, and Frank Longstreth, eds. 1992. *Structuring Politics: Historical Institutionalism in Comparative Analysis.* Cambridge: Cambridge University Press.

Stiglitz, Joseph E. 1994. *Whither Socialism?* Cambridge, MA: MIT Press.

Thelen, Kathleen, and Sven Steinmo. 1992. "Historical Institutionalism in Comparative Politics." In *Structuring Politics: Historical Institutionalism in Comparative Analysis,* ed. Sven Steinmo, Kathleen Thelen, and Frank Longstreth. Cambridge: Cambridge University Press.

Thompson, Dennis. 1987. *Political Ethics and Public Office.* Cambridge, MA: Harvard University Press.

Thompson, Michael, Richard Ellis, and Aaron Wildavsky. 1990. *Cultural Theory.* Boulder, CO: Westview Press.

Tilly, Charles. 1984. *Big Structures, Large Processes, Huge Comparisons.* New York: Russell Sage Foundation.

Toulmin, Stephen. 1958. *The Uses of Argument.* Cambridge: Cambridge University Press.

Toulmin, Stephen, and Albert Jonsen. 1988. *The Abuse of Casuistry: A History of Moral Reasoning.* Berkeley: University of California Press.

Vickers, Geoffrey. 1965. *The Art of Judgment: A Study of Policy Making.* London: Methuen.

Wade, Robert. 1990. *Governing the Market: Economic Theory and the Role of Government in East Asian Industrialization.* Princeton, NJ: Princeton University Press.

Walker, Jack L. 1977. "Setting the Agenda in the U.S. Senate." *British Journal of Political Science* 7 (October): 423–445.

Walton, Douglas N. 1992. *Plausible Argument in Everyday Conversation.* Albany: State University of New York Press.

Weaver, R. Kent, and Bert A. Rockman, eds. 1993. *Do Institutions Matter? Government Capabilities in the United States and Abroad.* Washington, DC: Brookings.

Weir, Margaret. 1992. "Ideas and the Politics of Bounded Innovation." In *Structuring Politics: Historical Institutionalism in Comparative Analysis,* ed. Sven Steinmo, Kathleen Thelen, and Frank Longstreth. Cambridge: Cambridge University Press.

White, Leonard. 1933. *Trends in Public Administration.* New York: McGraw Hill.

Whittington, Richard. 1993. *What Is Strategy—and Does It Matter?* London: Routledge.

Wildavsky, Aaron. 1979. *Speaking Truth to Power: The Art and Craft of Policy Analysis.* Boston: Little, Brown.

Wilks, Stuart. 1996. "Sweden." In *Public Sector Management in Europe,* ed. Norman Flynn and Franz Strehl. Hemel Hempstead, England: Prentice Hall.

Willoughby, William F. 1918. *The Movement for Budgetary Reform in the States.* New York: D. Appleton.

Wilson, James Q. 1989. *Bureaucracy: What Government Agencies Do and Why They Do It.* New York: Basic Books.

Yeatman, Anna. 1987. "The Concept of Public Management and the Australian State in the 1980s." *Australian Journal of Public Administration* 46 (4): 339–353.

Zifcak, Spencer. 1994. *New Managerialism: Administrative Reform in Whitehall and Canberra.* Buckingham, England: Open University Press.

Subject Index

NAME INDEX

Compositor: Impressions Book and Journal Services, Inc.
Text: 10/15 Janson
Display: Syntax Bold
Printer: Rose Printing Company, Inc.
Binder: Rose Printing Company, Inc.